D1546871

Chosen Faith, Chosen Land

The Untold Story of America's 21st-Century Shakers

Chosen Faith, Chosen Land

The Untold Story of America's 21st-Century Shakers

Jeannine Lauber

Down East

Copyright © 2009 by Story Productions, LLC
All rights reserved.
www.chosenfaithchosenland.com
Unless otherwise noted, all photographs by Jeff Toorish
All other illustrations, unless otherwise noted, courtesy of Sabbathday Lake Shaker Community

ISBN (13-digit): 978-0-89272-811-4

Library of Congress Cataloging-in-Publication Data

Lauber, Jeannine, 1955-
  Chosen faith, Chosen Land : the untold story of America's 21st century Shakers / by Jeannine Lauber.
     p. cm.
  Includes bibliographical references (p.   ) and index.
  ISBN 978-0-89272-811-4 (trade hardcover : alk. paper)
  1. Shakers--Maine--Sabbathday Lake. 2. Sabbathday Lake (Me.)--Religious life and customs. I. Title.
  BX9768.S2L38 2009
  289'.8090511--dc22
                          2009025082

Design by Lynda Chilton

Printed in China.

5 4 3 2 1

www.downeast.com
Distributed to the trade by National Book Network

Dedication

To my children, Christian and Tyler, who traveled for more than a decade with me to Chosen Land, where we all enjoyed the freedom to explore a different perspective on the image and nature of God. And to Mark, who took care of everything while I followed the leading of the Spirit.

Contents

Foreword

by Gerard C. Wertkin

Throughout the years of their long and storied presence in America, the Shakers have gathered together in families of shared faith and common interest. This is as true today, when only one Shaker family survives, as it was when many hundreds of Believers—women, men, and children—lived out consecrated lives of work and worship in each of twenty-six principal communities. Despite its small numbers, the last Shaker family, with but three covenanted members, continues in the ways of the faith at Sabbathday Lake, Maine, a place of simple grace and unexpected liveliness, where Shakers have cleaved to the land for well over two hundred years. In this engaging volume, Jeannine Lauber introduces today's Shakers and opens the door to a fuller understanding of their daily lives in the context of their history and principles. Importantly, she invites the Shakers to speak for themselves, and they do so with remarkable candor, insight, and spiritual discernment.

In the mid-nineteenth century, during a period of intense religious revival among the Believers, each Shaker community adopted a spiritual name. Sabbathday Lake became known as "Chosen Land," an especially fitting designation that remains in regular use among the Shakers today. Although each of the three remaining Sabbathday Lake Shakers—Eldress Frances Carr, Brother Arnold Hadd, and Sister June Carpenter—took a distinctively different path to Shakerism, each chose this place and this way of life. Through a series of sensitive, even intimate, interviews with her subjects, the author traces the routes taken by each member of the family to a life's home and fulfillment at Chosen Land.

The nation's last three Shakers do not labor alone in their work or in the practices of their faith. As these pages reveal, a host of friends and associates support their efforts, volunteer in various community departments, or regularly participate in their church services. Some may even try the Shaker life as members of the community's novitiate. They are part of an extended Shaker family that stretches across the country and beyond its borders. But there is another, more profound, reason why these latter-day Believers do not feel alone in their daily rounds. They often recall, as a living reality, the encouraging words of Jesus: "For when two or three are gathered together in my name, there am I in the midst of them (Matthew 18:20)." It is this certainty of the divine presence among them that sustains the little family, and grounds it in its Christian faith.

The evocative photographs that help tell this story underscore the quiet dignity and natural beauty of the nation's last active Shaker village. Indeed, Sabbathday Lake has been recognized as a national treasure and a landmark of architecture and design. But it is much more than a historic site or museum. As the home of generations of Believers, it is a place of authentic spirituality and Christian witness. The Shaker family that occupies its impressive buildings is faithful to traditional ways, but still has new contributions to make. As Jeannine Lauber illustrates so well in *Chosen Faith, Chosen Land,* the Shakers look with confidence to the future even as they preserve their past.

Preface

I met Sister Frances Carr, the leader of America's Shakers, fifteen years ago, after my first Sunday Meeting at Chosen Land, near Sabbathday Lake, in rural Maine. I soaked in every detail of the service, from the selection of Scripture to the wide wooden planks of the floor, from the way the two Shaker men sat on the opposite side of the large, high-ceilinged room as the three Shaker women, to the way the outside world looked slightly different through the antique panes of glass on the double-hung windows. I made special note of the way the dozen or so non-Shaker participants joined in with their thoughts midway through the service. I sat silent that Sunday morning, thinking, watching, letting my feelings wash over me.

It was unlike anything I had ever experienced. I come from a Catholic upbringing, and it seemed odd to me that there were no crucifixes or stained-glass windows, no organ music, no clerical robes. Most remarkable was the fact that nearly everyone, even non-Shakers, participated with equal authority. I wondered what it would feel like to stand up and "testify" in front of others. I wondered if people thought about what they would say before the service, or if their words were more spontaneous.

After the service everyone moved into an adjoining room where we greeted each other and exchanged pleasantries. Sister Frances was in her mid-60s back then. She had a charming wide smile and a natural talent for making people feel at ease. She looked beautiful in her royal blue Shaker dress. She extended her hand for me to shake and asked, "How is it that you came here today?"

I answered that I was new in town and had mentioned to a neighbor that I was looking for a church to attend. "And what a coincidence," I said. "My neighbor is one of your summer tour guides, and she thought I might enjoy it here."

I'll never forget what Sister Frances said next: "There are no coincidences in life, dear, only God-incidences." She wasn't making small talk. She said it as though it was a fact. And with a firm nod indicating the end of our brief introduction, she let go of my hand. Her words, few as they were, had a profound effect on me.

I knew I would return to Chosen Land, and I did. I needed to know more about this faith that, at first glance, I found so appealing. I soon became a "regular," one of about three dozen or so local people who worship often with the Shakers.

Sister Frances Carr reads one of her favorite Shaker poems, "Mother's Mission," to author Jeannine Lauber during a break from filming in 2003.

Back in those days, I was working as a prime-time anchor and reporter for the ABC News affiliate in Portland. I was proud of my work, especially my investigative pieces, and I was well suited to big, complicated stories. I was also something of a local celebrity and the Shakers occasionally teased me about it. My picture sometimes appeared on the sides of busses during the "ratings season," and on one occasion Sister Frances jokingly said, "I waved to you today while I was out shopping, Jeannine, but you just zipped right by!" I was comfortable with my church family, and they seemed equally comfortable with me.

Maybe that was why, a few years later, Sister Frances pulled me aside after meeting and asked, "Is there anything you can do to get PBS to stop airing their documentary about us?" She was talking about Ken Burns's *The Shakers: Hands to Work, Hearts to God.* "It's full of mistakes and gives people the impression there are no Shakers left, that our faith is dead." Her words spilled out like steam from a kettle. "I've called them several times," she told me, "but nobody calls back. I even wrote a letter, but no one even bothered to respond."

Clearly this had been bothering her for a long time. I knew of the Ken Burns documentary; he had, indeed, made a mistake, one that chipped away at the viability of the Shaker faith every time it aired. But how could I help?

"Sister," I began, "there's no way I can get PBS to drop programming. If they won't listen to you, they surely won't listen to me." I paused to collect my thoughts. "But, what I can do, with your help, is tell people the real story about the Shakers. I can do my own documentary. It may not be as popular as Ken Burns's film, but I promise to do my best to tell the truth about what's happening here."

And that's how it began. I started working on the story in October 2000. My goal was twofold: to tell the story of a simple people trying to live God's will as they see it, and to shatter the tragic misperception that America's Shakers, and their faith, are dead. It was a challenge like none I had ever faced before. There were budgets to create, reports to fill out, research to do, phone calls to make, people to hire, scholars to consult—all things requiring an enormous amount of time and money. There would be no employer behind me this time. The burden of setting the record straight sat squarely on my shoulders.

I got to work right away writing grants seeking funding. Within a year I had enough money to film the Shakers' oral histories and hold a scholar seminar to help guide my research prior to the shoot. I was well on my way when the unthinkable happened. I was seriously injured in an automobile accident and had to stop working. I spent nine months at an outpatient rehabilitation facility and underwent surgery to repair my failing eyesight. "The Shaker Project" was stalled for more than a year. I wondered if the story would ever be told. I couldn't do it alone anymore. I prayed for help. Then, one day, a writer and emerging filmmaker who had heard about my project called. Her name is Betsy Connor Bowen. She told me of her lifelong curiosity about the Shakers and her admiration for the faith. We agreed to collaborate. That was a "God-incident," for sure.

And so in the fall of 2003, Betsy and I, and a crew of seven, spent a week at Chosen Land interviewing the Shakers. Their responses and images, captured on video and in more than 1,800 photographs, are the basis for this book and a planned documentary film with the same title. The Shakers did not ask me to do this, but they participated fully.

During the year that followed I made a remarkable discovery. As I researched the Shaker faith within the spectrum of American Christianity, I learned of an amazing new faith that was growing by leaps and bounds—

The author directs documentary filming at Chosen Land in 2003.

due in large part to the Internet. It's called the "Postmodern" or "Emerging" Christian church. It began popping up on the radar screens of religious scholars in the early 1990s, although the movement itself dates back to at least the early 1980s. What fascinated me most were the dramatic similarities between Postmodernism and Shakerism. My instinct as an investigative reporter kicked in. Could I prove that America's oldest religion resembled its newest? And if I could, what meaning would it hold?

Postmodern Christians, I learned, feel that faith should be more than just believing in something, it's about doing something; it's about the way you live, and about being responsible for the choices you make. Postmodern Christians also believe faith is about doing the work of salvation yourself, rather than adopting someone else's creed, theology, or spirituality. Both groups believe faith is a very individual experience.

Postmodernists, like Shakers, are perennially in search of life's meaning by living "lives with meaning." They are politically active. They buy and think "green." They are religiously and socially tolerant. They are also non-hierarchal in structure, as are Shakers. They particularly shun the "mega-churches" of the 1980s and 90s in favor of smaller, more intimate gatherings where worship and religious discussion are less structured. They would likely feel right at home in a Shaker Meeting House, also known as a "house church."

As you learn more about today's Shakers, you may ask who are the Postmodernists? They are described by scholars as being mostly young, liberal, educated, Internet-savvy Christians who reject traditional churches in pursuit of a new and deeper understanding of the image and nature of God. Likewise,

Ann Lee, who established the Shaker faith, also rejected her traditional church and its image of God. She and her early followers paid a dear price for their radical departure from the religious norm.

Where did all this lead me? I concluded with firm conviction that the rapidly emerging Postmodern Christian faith is essentially a mirror image of America's Shaker faith; that Shakerism, far from being "over" (when measured exclusively by membership), is alive and well by virtue of the fact that the faith itself (the true measure) reflects something quite vibrant. Even if the day comes when there are no Shakers, the heart and soul of their faith will remain alive in the people who comprise the Postmodern movement that now spans the globe. It is a conclusion I could never have predicted.

Nor could I have predicted how coming to know the Shakers would change me. I matured spiritually, and I began to look at the world differently. I became tolerant and much more ecumenical about the nature of worship. I found something good in everyone. I could see the spark. I changed my idea of the "image" of God. I began listening to my inner voice. I followed the leading of the Spirit. I don't recall exactly when all this happened, it wasn't an earth-shattering moment, but at one point I realized I had become a different woman. Shakerism had transformed me.

What I now realize is that this project is my public testimony. It is my prayer for peace and tolerance, my prayer that people will stop hurting each other in the name of God, my prayer that the Spirit, which is the essence of love, will be set free among us all. That is the real meaning of "Shaker style," and it feels good and right to share these feelings with you.

—Jeannine Lauber, Casco, Maine

The Spirit and the Bride

Is it over or just beginning?

Predawn mist rising off
Sabbathday Lake.

"I will pour out my Spirit upon all people. Your sons and daughters will prophesy. Your old men will dream dreams, your young men will see visions. In those days, I will pour out my Spirit even on servants - men and women alike."

JOEL 2:28-29

Mother Ann Lee (1736–1784), Founder

A fragment of 18th-century checked gingham, believed to be from the apron of America's first Shaker, Ann Lee (1736 –1784), rests upon the outstretched hands of Brother Arnold Hadd, a 21st-century Believer who is likely one of America's last Shakers. Brother Arnold represents a small but sturdy link in an unbroken chain of an estimated 70,000 Americans who spent all or part of their lives as Shakers during the faith's 225-year history.

*C*hosen Faith, Chosen Land is as much a story about Ann Lee, the woman who founded the Shaker faith in America in 1774, as it is about the living Shakers themselves.

The story the living Shakers tell is intimately woven into the story of a woman who followed her inner vision, and how that vision transformed their lives. The Shakers add first-person insight and meaning to the dramatic tale of how Ann Lee came to this country on the eve of the American Revolution to ignite a religious revolution within a political one, and then died from injuries suffered at the hands of angry mobs. She eventually triumphed, reemerging across time as a larger-than-life spiritual presence in their lives and those of Shakers past.

Most of what we know about Ann Lee comes from the 1816 *Testimonies,* a collection of first-person accounts from Shakers who actually knew her. These remembrances were gathered by Shaker scribes about twenty years after Ann Lee's death in 1784 in an effort to preserve her memory for generations to come. Through these stories we see reflected an early America that promised freedom of religion with one hand, but, while granting it, extracted with the other a severe price for practicing a faith deemed by many to be too far outside the religious norm. But by remaining alive in the Shaker faith, Ann Lee stands as testimony to the enduring democratic ideals, traditions, and achievements that can blossom in a nation that promises and then truly honors religious freedom.

Ann Lee's life matters because it was her belief in the "God within" that gave birth to the faith that inspired the Shaker movement. Equally American, she transplanted the faith to this country from England because of a vision that it would take root here and thrive. It did. It is a quintessential American success story. Shakers have outlasted all other similar communitarian experiments. They created an almost complete society based on their theological

One of only a few copies of a hand-written manuscript from a collection of first-hand rememberances of Mother Ann Lee. The full collection was published by the Shakers in 1816 as the *Testimonies Concerning The Character And Ministry of Mother Ann Lee.* The rare manuscript, cradled in the hands of Brother Arnold, is safely stored in the climate-controlled library at Chosen Land.

vision—architecture, industry, music, furniture, living arrangements, and social organization are but a few of the fundamentals for which they are so well noted. They stand, therefore, as a unique commentary on the rest of American society; grateful to be in America, but also grateful because they could separate from it. The American Shaker experience is a part of our history, a part we should not want to lose. If we fail to understand it, we are doomed to repeat mistakes from the past on new generations of radical religious thinkers.

When you focus on the Shaker faith, its connection to what religious scholar Elaine Pagels calls the "underground river" of religious ideas—often referred to as "Gnosticism"—reveals itself. "Gnosticism" is from a Greek word used to describe an esoteric "knowing" of a spiritual truth. Shakers hold to a way of "knowing" that directs their search for God not outwards but inwards, to the "Christ Spirit." In Gnostic terms it is defined as the Divine "spark" encased in each individual. Ann Lee passionately believed the Divine spark, which she called the Christ Spirit, could "dwell within the consciousness of any man, woman, or child." Access to God, she felt, is non-hierarchal and available to all because it is found within.

Harold Bloom, Sterling Professor of Humanities at Yale, in *The American Religion* (1992) draws a direct connection between Shakerism and Gnosticism. Using the term in a broad sense, Bloom's controversial view is that religions founded on American soil have been pervasively Gnostic, the Shakers being the first. He writes, "Ann Lee's vision of God essentially was Gnostic, and followed the ancient concept that God was both our fore-mother and our fore-father, both female and male. In America, the Shaker founder went further, and soon was regarded by her followers as a female Jesus, and became known as Mother Ann Lee, in a relation both divine and maternal. Though all Shakers, and not just Mother Ann, incarnated the Spirit, they became in effect an extended family, all of them her children. The gifts of the Spirit were thus

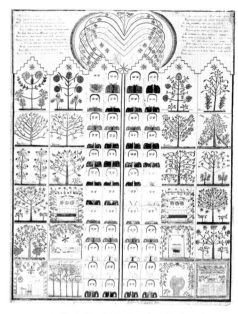

Polly Collins' gift drawing depicts the saints in Heaven who have benefited humanity with their moral goodness. The top row, from left to right, consists of Ann Lee, founder of the Shaker faith in America, 1774, Father James Whittaker, successor to Ann Lee; Father William Lee, Ann Lee's brother; and Christopher Columbus. The second row consists of "The Savior" (Jesus Christ): Saints Peter, Andrew, and James the Lesser. Polly Collins, 1854, Hancock, Massachusetts. Courtesy of Hancock Shaker Village, Pittsfield, Massachusetts

Miranda Barber's depiction of Ann Lee on the cross, from her "Book of Prophetic Signs Written by Prophet Isaiah" (Mt. Lebanon, 1843), summons up a powerful body of lore shaped by previous generations of Shakers. This single image would have evoked the many parallels between Ann Lee's life and Jesus's, of which death by persecution was only one, albeit the most powerful. Appearing from the Spirit World bearing the comforting words, "I never will forsake thee," Barber's vision granted a new generation of Shakers needed unity with their spiritual mother. Detail from "A Book of prophetic signs written by Prophet Isaiah, 1843," by Miranda Barber, Mt. Lebanon, New York, 198 pages; ink, watercolor and graphite on paper, leather-bound. Pages size: 8 1/2 x 6 13/16 in. Courtesy of The Western Reserve Historical Society, Cleveland, Ohio

both singular and familial, and an odd blend of individualism and communalism had been created."

Today's Shakers do not agree with Bloom's entire theory, pointing out that Ann Lee never talked about belief in a Father/Mother God, nor did she consider herself a female Jesus, even though others did. Regardless, Ann Lee had never heard the word "gnostic," but she saw in an intuitive flash that breaking loose from the bonds of the flesh (celibacy) could free the individual to be closer to God, closer to the "inner light." By seeking the "sparks" within, we find God and grow closer to the Spirit. Hence to be a Shaker is to search one's self in pursuit of the elusive inner light, the knowledge of God. For Ann Lee, it was necessary for the individual to break loose from the flesh to get there. Celibacy has been part of Shakerism from the beginning, and it remains so today.

Forsaking the flesh would never become a mainstream American vision. What did become mainstream, however, was the *direction* of Ann Lee's seeking. Bloom writes, "Awareness, centered on the self, is *faith* for the American Religion. . . . Emerson, writing in his journal in 1831, gave his nation one of its prime statements of its spiritual peculiarities:

> Remember, then, were not the words that made your blood run cold, that brought the blood to your cheeks, that made you tremble or delighted you—did they not sound to you as old as yourself? Was it not truth that you knew before, or do you ever expect to be moved from the pulpit or from man by anything but plain truth? Never. It is God in you that responds to God without, or affirms his own words trembling on the lips of another."

Bloom continues, "The self is the truth, and there is a spark at its center that is best and oldest, being the God within."

If America is now, as appears to be the case, taking a renewed look at "the

God within," and if Ann Lee is among America's religious leaders who first brought such an idea to these shores, maybe the more important question is not whether the Shaker faith is about to end, but whether it is just beginning to undergo a worldwide revival...under a different name.

I believe people are ready to take a serious look at the Shaker faith, and the untold story of Ann Lee is a good place to start. Not only are the living Shakers willing to tell her story, but new scholarship is available and the American psyche may at last be ripe for it, as well. Why? Religion has entered our political arena, for better or worse. We live in an America where religious diversity is increasing, and the possibility for persecution and violence is ever-present. Faith is at the forefront of our collective consciousness. It can be so deeply personal, so irrational, that it can be the cause of the most noble and most ignoble human behavior. It can inflame us, in good ways and in bad.

Like the lives of so many other religious leaders, Ann Lee's life moves from hope to despair to renewed faith. It is one of early religious seeking solidifying into rock-solid conviction, the courage to follow inner direction wherever it might go, daring leadership, persistence in the face of seeming defeat, a fast-growing following igniting vicious persecution, early death at the hands of enemies, and resurrection as a spiritual presence to generations who had never known her in the flesh.

Ultimately, this is a story about a woman reaching across time to lead new generations of unconventional religious thinkers into the future.

"We are the people who turn the world upside down." —Ann Lee

Ann Lee was born into a working-class family in 1736 in Manchester, England. Her father was a blacksmith. Her mother's name was never recorded.

Ann was expected to work even as a child and she did. Her first job, at only eight years old, was in a cotton factory. She was unschooled and illiterate, but those who knew her as a child say she was bright and very curious. Ann's mother was reportedly passionate about religion, an interest she shared with her daughter, who was also eager to "know" spiritual truths.

England at that time was in the grip of a hotbed of religious enthusiasm known as the "First Great Awakening." This controversial revival, a Protestant reform movement that also swept Germany, Scotland, and the American colonies, stressed trusting the heart rather than the head in spiritual matters. "Feelings" were prized more highly than "thinking," and spiritual seekers were encouraged to rely on Biblical revelation rather than human reasoning. It was a "new age" religion and people flocked to it, abandoning their traditional churches en masse.

It was also an era of extraordinary social and political upheaval affecting the lives of ordinary people. England was struggling with the transition into the Industrial Revolution. Northern Ireland and Germany were wracked by war and famine. Colonialists' hardscrabble lives were constantly threatened by attacks from dispossessed Native Americans. What occurred was a "perfect storm" involving several unstable fronts, from social to economic and cultural to political, that collided then erupted with the births of several radical new breeds of old religions. One example is the Methodist Church, which grew out of a movement to reform the Anglican Church of England in the 18th century.

This was the atmosphere in 1758, when 22-year-old Ann Lee joined the Wardley Society, a small radical offshoot of the English Methodists that practiced open confession and ecstatic worship. The "shaking" they did during religious meetings was considered a sign that the Spirit dwelt within them. To outsiders, most particularly members of the established Church of England, it was a sign of something else, and Believers were routinely ridiculed and persecuted. They were derisively called the "Shaking Quakers," (Believers were often confused with Quakers, but research points to Methodist roots), a term later shortened to "Shakers" when they came to this country.

In 1762, at the age of 26, Ann Lee married Abraham Standerin, a blacksmith who worked in her father's shop. Some records indicate Ann was forced into the marriage. We'll never know whether that is true or not, but records confirm the couple had four children, three of whom died in infancy. Their daughter Elizabeth died at the age of six. Ann was emotionally devastated by the deaths of her children, and may have suffered what we know of today as a major clinical depression. Of that traumatic time in her life she later told followers:

> I felt my soul overwhelmed with sorrow. In my travail and tribulation my sufferings were so great that my flesh consumed upon my bones, bloody sweat pressed through my skin, and I became helpless as an infant. And when I was brought through and born into the spiritual kingdom, I was like an infant just brought into the world. They see works and colors and objects but they know not what they see, and so it was with me when I was brought into the spiritual world. But before I was twenty-four hours old, I saw and knew what I saw.

Critics of Ann Lee say the untimely deaths of her children is probably what prompted her eventual belief that sex was spiritually evil, that she most likely felt the deaths were her punishment for engaging in carnal activity. Her followers strongly disagree, arguing Ann Lee's position on the nature and spiritual consequences of human sexuality came to her through Divine inspiration. What we know is that Ann Lee left her husband's bed, that he adamantly opposed her total rejection of sex, and that he even complained about his wife to local clergy, all to no avail. What is less understood is why Abraham remained with Ann for several years, even joining the tiny band of eight Believers who followed her on a dangerous journey across the Atlantic to America. Early Shaker literature offers little to help understand their relationship, which by all accounts ended a few years after they arrived in America.

The early 1770s marked a time of social and spiritual maturation for Ann Lee. Like many before, she had become extremely disillusioned with the Church of England. She publicly accused its hierarchy of choreographing a despicable "trickle-down" structure where God was at the top; then the monarch; then nobles; and at the bottom were the common people. Her vision for a new gospel and a new order, she later said, would "turn the world upside down." It did. She preached that the Christ Spirit could come into the life of anyone, directly, from within. There was no need for the Church as mediator, because the Church itself is the body of Christ, welcoming anyone ready to receive the Spirit.

"As a young woman she began taking up her cause against the Anglican Church," says Sister Frances. "And she took it upon herself to do something unheard of in that day." Ann Lee burst into church services, disrupted worship, and publicly accused the clergy of ignoring the poor and catering to the wealthy. To break from England's established religion was one thing, but for a woman to lead a reform involving deliberately hostile and confrontational tactics was quite another.

"That took a lot of doing in those days," says Sister Frances.

"She went into state churches and started telling people they were damned, that they weren't getting the message, that they weren't really worshiping God," says Brother Wayne.

"She had the example of Jesus the Christ going in and upsetting the temple, and I think that gave her courage," says Sister Frances. "She had that same spirit within her. She knew she would suffer for it and indeed she did."

And so began a vicious cycle of religious protest, followed by imprisonment, persecution, and violence for Ann Lee and her followers. One of the most horrific prison incidents occurred in 1770 after Ann Lee, her father, and a few other followers boldly protested Divine Services at Christ Church in Manchester. The radicals, well known to authorities by now, were brought before Ecclesiastical authorities on charges of disrupting the Sabbath. They were thrown into jail at the Manchester House of Corrections. Ann Lee's cell was so small she couldn't even stand up. She was a lightening rod in a country where church and state were one.

"They sentenced her to prison for a long time, feeling it would either change her, or kill her," says Brother Arnold of the disease-ridden House of Corrections and the life-threatening conditions at the prison to which she was subjected.

"She was given nothing to eat or drink," says Sister Frances, "but one of her followers, James Whittaker, came and fed her through a straw that he put into the keyhole. That strengthened her so she didn't die of starvation."

"And during that time," explains Brother Arnold, "there was absolutely nothing she could do. She was already a person given over to intense prayer, and she had for years been supplicating God for answers, for a deeper conviction of faith, and for a way out of sin."

It was during this confinement that Ann Lee began to have visions. The Testimonies record she felt Christ was teaching her. One of her revelations concerned original sin. "She saw Adam and Eve in the Garden of Eden and realized where original sin came from," says Brother Arnold. He explains that Ann Lee concluded humanity loses its relationship with God through carnal relations, but that we could restore the relationship by forsaking the marriage of the flesh. "She was adamant about that," says Brother Arnold. "But what's interesting is there's a flip side to it. There are a couple of Testimonies where she says, 'Do not go away and say that we don't believe in marriage. It's fine if you cannot live this life. It's better for man to cleave to a woman and to live true to her, and to her alone. That is the least sin.' "

Manchester House of Corrections, England. Circa 1770. Ann Lee was imprisoned here for 13 days in 1772. It was one of many occasions when she was locked up for boldly disturbing church services, flagrantly preaching against the Church of England, and a variety of other acts committed in defiance of religious mores.

TESTIMONIES

CONCERNING

THE CHARACTER AND MINISTRY OF

MOTHER ANN LEE

AND THE FIRST WITNESSES OF THE GOSPEL OF

CHRIST'S SECOND APPEARING:

GIVEN BY SOME OF THE AGED BRETHREN AND SISTERS
OF THE

Detail of the title page of the 1816
Testimonies.

Brother Wayne explains another important vision she had while imprisoned. "She had revelations that Christ's second appearing was not something that would happen as a great physical return on clouds of righteousness. But rather, Christ's second appearing would be within the church. That within the church we manifest that same indwelling presence of God that Jesus manifested in his life. She realized that we could truly become like Christ, (and) that we all could become brothers and sisters to the Christ as was intended."

Ann Lee reportedly astonished her jailers when she came out of her cell two weeks later, emerging upright, confident, and in apparent good health. "They thought she'd be at least crippled, but she wasn't. It was a miracle she was so preserved," says Brother Arnold of the fourteen days Ann Lee spent in the cramped cell in a cold stone prison. Wasting no time, she rushed to Manchester, where the Shakers were headquartered, and told them about her incredible spiritual revelations. "Almost on the spot they announced her to be the new leader (of the Wardley Society,)" Brother Arnold says, adding that it was also when Ann Lee came to be known as, "Mother" Ann, or "Our Mother in the New Creation."

He goes on to explain, "and in their understanding of what is Christ, it is the Spirit that inhabited Mother Ann that allowed her to do the miraculous things she did, and gather up all those thousands of people to the living way. That's the moment when they began to understand that she represented the second appearance of Christ." It would be several years before the concept would become fully realized by the earliest Shakers, nonetheless, it is considered a monumental turning point for the faith, setting it dramatically apart from all other Christian religions of that day.

As Brother Wayne explains it, they "truly felt she was Jesus Christ reincarnated." The early English Shakers believed the Christ Spirit had manifested itself a second time in the body of a woman—equalizing the gender issue. Believers would later aptly name their church The United Society of Believers in Christ's Second Appearance. Their unconventional belief in a "second appearance" in a female form forced late 18th- and early 19th-century Shakers to redefine their attitudes toward the role of women, their power and status. The Shaker belief system, to say the least, was far more serious at that time than any other religion regarding the issue of women being full citizens of heaven *and* earth.

Today's Shakers, like their predecessors dating back to the middle period of Shakerism, do not believe Ann Lee represents the Second Coming of Christ. They cite their founder's own words, as recorded in the *Testimonies*, as evidence: "It is not I that do these things, but the Christ Spirit that is in me." The disconnect among early Shakers, according to Brother Wayne, was because so many 18th-century people who were drawn to Ann Lee were so caught up in the fervor of The Great Awakening, and were actually looking for the physical manifestation of the Second Coming, that they believed they saw it happening within Ann Lee. Brother Wayne feels this country's first Shakers were probably so preoccupied with literal Biblical interpretations that they actually missed Ann Lee's point, "that the indwelling presence of God, the anointing Spirit that made Jesus the Christ, can be manifested in all of us. That's truly what the message of her revelation was," he says.

Not long after, Mother Ann and a few other Shakers began to have visions about coming to America. John Hocknell, the wealthiest Shaker, was asked to find a ship and book passage. The only ship he could find was condemned, and when he told this to Mother Ann she replied, "God would not condemn it when we were in it."

So passage was booked and they set sail aboard the *Mariah* on May 19, 1774. Mother Ann was joined by her rejected husband, her brother William (a former Royal Calvary officer), her niece, Nancy Lee, a young weaver named James Whittaker (who had fed her through the keyhole when she was in prison in Manchester, who would later succeed her in leadership) and John

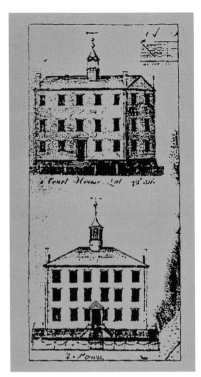

1794 drawing of the court house and prison at Albany, New York, where Mother Ann was tried and jailed.

Hocknell, the man who has booked the vessel, James Shepherd, Mary Partington, and Richard Hocknell.

On August 6, 1774, two-and-a-half months after setting sail from England, they arrived in New York. Mother Ann had brought a revolutionary new faith to a new country on the eve of its Revolutionary War. Their mission was to bring souls to salvation, for "the Kingdom" had come, and you could find it by searching inward, by forsaking the flesh, and following the path of peace. Stories about the group of religious radicals soon spread like wildfire. Her followers, "filled with the Spirit," shook and trembled wildly and spoke in tongues. Ann Lee could reportedly see into people's hearts and minds; send shock waves through them, even perform miracles. Her newly converted Believers were unswerving in their certainty of salvation.

"The first generation of Believers in America was very Biblically centered and, like so many people of their time, they were convinced the end of the world was imminent," says Brother Arnold of the Shaker's Millenialist position. "They were searching for the time and the circumstances when this was going to happen, which led them to a lot of obscure texts. Not so obscure is the Book of Revelation. In it you have these allusions to the woman who is "clothed in the sun," and the Believers very early on equated Mother Ann with that woman, who was protected by God, taken into the wilderness (which they equated with the period Mother Ann lived in Watervliet or Niskayuna, New York), and from thence would the Gospel be spread. Furthermore, there are constant allusions to Christ and his bride, the bride being the church, so they saw Mother Ann representing the church itself, as being the bride of Christ."

Brother Arnold says the Shaker concept of "the Spirit and the bride" has evolved somewhat, but still stands solid as it relates to the "fullness" of the biblical message "to bring about the new heaven and the new earth. And that's living the Millennium," he adds.

Ann Lee's message and her mission to save souls in America ignited as much persecution here as in the country she'd fled. There was no such thing as religious freedom in Colonial America. The country was engaged in a war with Britain, and the Shakers with their English accents were suspected of being spies. Worse yet, their leader was a woman who encouraged the breaking of the bonds of the natural family by creating spiritual families. A conversion to their faith might result in a wifeless husband, a husbandless wife, children separated from their natural parents. There was also the issue of scarcity. Colonials accused Shakers of coming into a community and buying up all the grain to feed their growing ranks of converts, driving up prices.

Shaker evangelism threatened mainstream local churches. As Ann Lee's movement grew, disaffected converts ("apostates") began to publish anti-Shaker tracts accusing them of immorality and coercion. To Believers, Mother Ann Lee was a redeemer, but to many others she was a witch, a whore, and a man dressed in woman's clothing.

"Mother and the Elders were a primary target because they refused to pledge allegiance to the United States because," says Brother Arnold. "She tried to tell them (the Colonialists) that whether they took an oath or not they were well wishers to the country, but people were too hyped up. That was one of the reasons why Mother was frequently stripped to prove that she was a woman because many people felt that she was actually a man, and that she was a British spy. All these things caused her no end of physical pain, but even greater sufferings in her mind."

"I suspect when they left the Old World, they had no concept that America could be on a par with England. They were wrong. It was worse. They were far more vicious," says Brother Arnold. Ironically, Mother Ann tried to avoid persecution in this country by not taking the same tact that she took in England. She did not disrupt religious services. But her message was a new idea that frightened many people on multiple levels from social to economic and Biblical to political. Add to that an English accent and it's no wonder America's first Shakers were whipped, stoned, and violated. But the Shakers never struck back, and their abusers were always forgiven.

Their pacifism was rooted in the desire to live as the early apostles had. Frontier mobs, however, called for more than "turning the other cheek." They called for strategy, and slowly Mother Ann developed one. She avoided population centers and staying too long in one place. When a mob would assemble and threaten, increasingly she would speak to the crowd and try to reason with people. Sometimes when mobs lingered all night Mother Ann would invite them in for breakfast and pray with them. In these and many other practical ways, she taught pacifism. Sometimes she was successful. Sometimes she was not.

The most violent persecutions occurred in the early 1780s in Massachusetts. Brother Arnold tells the story of a particularly brutal attack in Petersham after Mother Ann had gone to bed. "One late night a mob broke down the door and began going room to room. The Shakers didn't want them to find Mother, so they put out the candles so no one could see who was there. They did everything in their power to hide her, but they weren't successful. The mob got her and dragged her down the stairs like a corpse, and her head hit every single step.

"Then several of the men picked her up and threw her into a sleigh. Her followers weren't going to take this lying down. They surrounded the sleigh trying to rescue Mother. Father James (Whittaker) got ahold on her, but one of the men beat him with a staff so violently around the head that he was thrown down, knocked unconscious and gushing blood. He broke some ribs as well, and when he finally revived, he dragged himself off to the barn. He had only been able to get ahold of Mother's cap, and he sat down and wept bitterly because that's the best he could do.

"Meanwhile, one of the Sisters managed to work her way in to be with Mother, and they start beating her about the head. She tried to provide protection to Mother, and a couple of other Sisters ran up on the sides. Then the Brethren got on their horses and chased down the mob. The mob managed to get to a tavern where they quickly convened a 'court' to convict Mother as an enemy of the state, and they actually did it. The next morning, the Shakers were able to win Mother's release. When she got home she showed the sisters all of the bruising, and she saw Father James with his broken ribs and torn clothing. And what did they do after that horrible ordeal? They had a joyful meeting to praise God and thank Him for her release."

Today's Shakers believe that Mother Ann never truly recovered from the injuries she sustained that night in Petersham. Her health began to fail, she retreated to her bed for long periods of time, and she eventually died. They believe Mother Ann, like Jesus Christ, was martyred for preaching her beliefs.

"I believe the violence ended her life," concludes Brother Arnold. "She enjoyed those last few months in relative peace, but they had already done their work. And certainly, when they exhumed her body to move it to the new cemetery, they found the fractured skull, which verified the fact that she died a slow, painful death. I believe she knew she was dying. And as is so often the case, all that persecution actually brought her more notoriety, and in the end brought more converts, but it sadly cost her her life, too."

After her death, James Whittaker assumed leadership and gathered small groups of Shakers across New England into order, persuading them to live together in community. He died three years later, in 1787.

After Whittaker's death, Joseph Meacham became the leader of the Shakers. Ever the practical man, he designed Shaker villages to be "heavens on earth," mirrors of the Spirit world, but also to become highly efficient, economically successful units that would keep Shakers apart from the world while giving them the means to support growing numbers. He then did what Ann Lee had resisted doing: he wrote and published for "the world" a theological summary of the Shaker faith. His *Concise Statement* makes no mention of Ann Lee.

Mother Ann Lee's final resting place at the "Common Burying Ground" in Albany, New York, near Watervliet, the site of the first Shaker Community (1776.) Mother's body was moved here in 1835, during which time an "examination of the relics of Mother Ann" revealed her fractured skull. It is proof, say Shakers, that she died a martyr for the faith. The tiny stones placed on her grave are a tribute to her honor to, by proving her final resting place is visited.

Mother Ann Lee's original hand-carved marble headstone rests in peace against a 2nd-floor wall in the Herb House at Chosen Land. It was brought here "about 30 years ago," recalls Brother Arnold, because it "had become so worn down" that it had to be removed and replaced. Stored in the most unassuming of places, its placement a testimony to the fact that Shakerism truly puts no faith in the material world, opting instead for monuments found in heaven. Her headstone reads, "Mother Ann Lee, Born in Manchester, England Feb. 29, 1736; Died Watervliet, New York Sept. 8, 1784.

Meacham instituted dual-gendered governance. He placed at his side Lucy Wright, an early convert whom Ann Lee had sanctioned. When she acceded to leadership, she ordered the collecting of first-hand accounts of Mother Ann from those who had known her—a timely move considering this was a generation advanced in years. These were stories that had been kept alive within the community, but had never been put into print. They were gathered into the *Testimonies* (1816) and twenty copies were published to be distributed among the communities.

Then, unexpectedly, amidst growing concern amongst Shaker leadership that a new generation was growing up not knowing their "Mother," came the "Era of Manifestations" (1837–1850) when "instruments," mainly young women, reported seeing Mother in the spirit world through trance-induced vision. Mother's gifts were poetry, music, and drawings. These were announced and shared in the community, just as Mother Ann had shared her visions. They reanimated Shaker spirituality. Mother lived—but within the veiled secrecy of Shaker communities.

Shakers today no longer fear the physical persecution of their early history. But they have been the victims of a subtler disservice: media distortion and misunderstanding. That is why it is important to hear what they have to say, and get it right. Equally important is Ann Lee's message and the persecution it provoked. If freedom of religion is one of our founding principles, why was she beaten, humiliated, sexually assaulted repeatedly, and eventually died of injuries suffered at the hands of angry early American mobs?

By engaging with this question, we come closer to seeing our true selves: a nation with high ideals thrown into sharp relief by the shadows cast upon them. We must not fail to forget or understand.

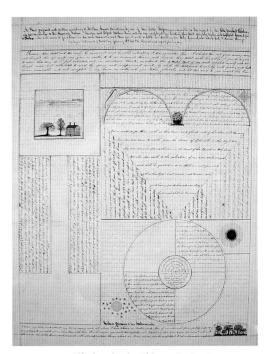

Gift drawing by Eldress Hester Ann Adams of Canterbury, New Hampshire. The mystical image is titled, "A sheet prepared & written According to Mother Ann's directions...Seen by instrument of Mortal Clay January 12, 1845 Sab. P.M. Received and copied following day." Ink and watercolor on paper, 20 ½ x 15 ¾ inches.

Like the Berkshire hills from where their earliest converts came, today's Shakers are old mountains. Once they were volcanoes spouting the kind of fire and brimstone sermons that defined the First Great Awakening, but time has weathered them. It has weathered them into a theological outlook not unlike a new "American religion" that some say defines the controversial Fourth Great Awakening. Exactly what degree of influence Shakers had in shaping the current face of our American religion is perhaps beyond knowing, but it is certain they had one.

Two hundred years ago, a great awakening occurred in the soul of an unlettered, impoverished Englishwoman that was so momentous she dedicated her life to sharing the spiritual message with others. Her name was Ann Lee. Word of her radical vision spread rapidly, and soon followers began flocking to her like doves. But she would be dead, murdered say some, within a few

This is the only photograph ever taken during an actual Shaker Sunday meeting. The 1885 professionally executed image came about because of a relationship the Chosen Land Shakers had cultivated with the nearby Ricker family of Poland, Maine. The Rickers owned and operated the Poland Spring Hotel, the site of the now famous mineral springs. The Shakers frequently visited the popular hotel, and the tourists, seated here in the back rows, frequently attended Shaker Sunday meeting.

Timeline:
The Shakers Through History

1730–1750 The First Great Awakening

1736 Ann Lee is born in Manchester, England.

1747 The Shakers as a distinct church are formed.

1758 Ann Lee joins the radical "Wardley Society" led by James and Jane Wardley. The sect believes in open confession and ecstatic worship. They are known derisively as the "Shaking Quakers."

1762 Ann Lee marries Abraham Standerin; they have four children, three of whom die during infancy; the fourth dies at six years of age.

1770 The Boston Massacre. British troops fire on a group of men and boys throwing snowballs and chunks of ice at them. Five are killed.

Ann Lee begins protesting the Church of England. She and her followers are routinely imprisoned. During one incarceration she claims to receive, through Divine Inspiration, teachings from the Spirit of Christ. Revelations follow. She is declared the new leader of the Shaking Quakers.

1773 Boston Tea Party. A group of protestors disguised as Indians dump tea worth 18,000 pounds sterling into Boston Harbor.

1774 Now called "Mother" Ann Lee, she and 8 Shakers arrive in New York to spread word of a "new gospel" and a "new order" in a new country.

1775 George Washington is selected Commander in Chief of the Continental Army.

The Battle of Bunker Hill.

The first anti-slavery society in the colonies is organized in Philadelphia.

1780 Mother Ann begins a public missionary tour to spread the message of Shakerism following the May 19th "Dark Day" in New England when the sun reportedly did not shine. The proselytizing is marked by renewed violence and persecution. Mother Ann and her followers are routinely accused, and occasionally imprisoned, of being British spies.

1782 Shakerism arrives in Maine. By the following year there are centers of union established in Alfred and Thompson's Pond Plantation (later New Gloucester).

1784 Ann Lee dies at the age of 48 in Watervliet (Niskayuna), New York. Her Millenialist gospel about Christ's Second Appearing had attracted the attention of thousands of people, many of whom converted to the Shaker life. She is succeeded by Father James Whittaker.

1787 Father James dies and is succeeded by Father Joseph Meacham. Under his direction the first Communities are gathered into Gospel Order: New Lebanon & Watervliet, New York.

1790–1840 The Second Great Awakening is marked in America by widespread Christian evangelism and conversion fostering participation in social causes and prompting reforms in areas such as prisons, slavery, and temperance.

1793 The first Shaker community in Maine is brought in "Gospel Order" in the town of Alfred.

1794 The second Shaker community in Maine is formally organized near Sabbathday Lake. It will later be given the "spiritual name" of CHOSEN LAND. This brings the total number of Shaker Villages in America to 11.

1837–1850 Mother Ann reemerges from the Spirit world during what is known as the "Era of Manifestations."

1840–1850 Shakerism reaches a zenith, with an estimated 5,000 Believers living in nearly two dozen villages around the United States.

1850–1900 The Third Great Awakening is characterized in America by postmillennial theology stating that the Second Coming of Christ would occur after mankind had reformed the entire earth. New religions emerge, such as the Church of the Nazarene and Christian Science.

1863 President Lincoln grants Shakers the right to refuse to fight in the Civil War. As pacifists, they are among the first people in America to be granted the status of "conscientious objector."

1870–1890 Membership begins to decline. Shaker communities begin closing.

1923 The American Shaker experience may have faded away virtually unnoticed had it not been for antiques dealers Edward Deming and Faith Andrews, who "discovered" Hancock Shaker Village in Pittsfield, Massachusetts. The couple began buying and selling Shaker furniture and other objects. They are credited with contributing greatly to the world's understanding and appreciation of Shaker material culture.

1931 The Shaker Community at Alfred, Maine, is closed due to financial problems and consolidates with the Shakers at Sabbathday Lake. Chosen Land is now the largest Shaker community.

1936 Only five active Shaker Villages remain.

1960–1980 The Fourth Great Awakening occurs. It is a controversial concept largely unsupported by mainstream scholars of American religion. However, there is general agreement that measurable changes did occur. Mainline Protestant churches weakened sharply in membership and influence. Schisms and theological battles erupted over the issues of abortion, gay rights, and creationism. The Christian Right was identified. Many churches actively sought political power. In response, newly styled non-denominational churches—"parachurches"—and community faith centers began to emerge. A global Pentecostal movement, that placed emphasis on the gifts of the Spirit, became one of the fastest growing movements in the history of modern Christianity.

1972 A schism occurs within the Shaker Church. The Maine Shakers refuse to follow the New Hampshire Shakers in closing membership, which would essentially end the faith. The Sabbathday Lake Shakers begin to reach out in an ecumenical spirit to the world and reopen Meeting to the public for the first time in more than eighty years. Today, people of all denominations worship together at Chosen Land.

1974 Chosen Land is designated a National Historic Landmark.

1992 Canterbury Shaker Village in New Hampshire closes with the death of the last Shaker living there. Today the site is one of fifteen Shaker Museums in the country at or near original Shaker Villages.

2007 Shakers raise nearly $3.7 million in an unprecedented nationwide effort that will preserve and protect Chosen Land forever.

2009 Chosen Land is America's only active Shaker Village, having survived longer (226 years to date) than any other village in the history of the Shaker church.

The Wisdom of Her Words

Labor to make the way of God your own. Let it be your inheritance, your treasure, your occupation, your daily calling.

You ought not to waste the least thing.

Be faithful with your hands, that you may have something to give to the poor.

You must not lose one moment of time, for you have none to spare.

Bring strength to the church, not weakness.

Never have one hard feeling towards each other, but live together every day as though it was the last you had to live in this world.

Never put on silver spoons nor tablecloths for me; but let your table be clean enough to eat from without cloths, and if you do not know what to do with them, give them to the poor.

Just in proportion as you heed the cries of the needy, God will heed yours.

If you improve in one talent, God will give you more.

Quell the spirit of fault finding; do not complain of the way of God until you have proved it; none ever thought it hard who were really in it.

Clean your room well, for good spirits will not live where there is dirt.
There is no dirt in heaven.

Do all your work as though you had a thousand years to live, and as you would if you knew you must die tomorrow.

Do not speak harshly, but let your words be few and seasoned with grace.

Hands to work, hearts to God.

—Mother Ann Lee, 1736–1784

The simple, yet beautiful nature of Shaker living can be seen even in the most unassuming of places at Chosen Land. Here, a wooden newel post and handrail elegantly offset the simple lines of a mustard yellow staircase.

years of the beginning of her public ministry. Two millennia ago, in another place, a prophet named Jesus also preached a profound spiritual message, one that was equally unorthodox, one that equally and quickly ignited a flame within the souls of thousands. He, too, was silenced for daring to question the nature of God.

In retrospect, it is not surprising that some called Ann Lee "The Second Coming of Christ." The year was 1774. The place was America. Her message echoed, then boldly advanced many of the philosophies spoken of by Jesus, her spiritual mentor. The movement she inspired swelled to a peak of 7,000 Believers in the mid-1800s who lived in two dozen utopian communities that stretched from Maine to Florida and west into Ohio and Kentucky. But now, in 2009, only three of Ann Lee's direct spiritual heirs remain. They live simple and quiet lives in a cluster of buildings that once bustled with the activities of rural New England life. Touched by the same Spirit that once embraced their founder, their 21st-century message echoes yet advances her original vision. They are what remain of America's Shakers.

It is a familiar story: A religious leader emerges, a message catches fire, a movement grows, then declines. A tangible line curves upwards, flattens out over time, then curves downward. So goes the tale many people tell of the American Shaker experience. But there remains an untold story that is far more important. A simple line cannot explain it. It is not so much the story of the rise and fall of a religious movement, but rather, the "movement" of a universal Spirit. From where did it come, and to where will it go? What is the shape of this Spirit? How can we speak of it? Or can we speak of it at all? To some it is like trying to measure the weight of the wind. But if anyone can give weight to the spiritual wind that blows out of the past, through them today, and into the future, it is America's living Shakers.

Sister Mildred Barker 1897–1990

No account of Shakerism in the 21st century would be complete or accurate without mention of Sister Mildred Barker and Brother Theodore "Ted" Johnson. These 20th-century Shakers fought many hard-won battles to keep the faith alive, setting the course for future promise. These two Believers, who traveled very different roads to Chosen Land, are primarily responsible for keeping the doors of the Shaker church open not only to new members but to the public, as well.

Mildred Barker was brought by her recently widowed mother to the Alfred, Maine, Shakers in 1904 and indentured to them. Her mother knew of the Shakers, as one of her nieces was already being raised there. She placed the rest of her children elsewhere. When Mildred was a teenager her mother

Sister Mildred Barker (1897–1990) at Chosen Land circa 1965 with her beloved dog "Lady." Copyright John Loengard.

returned to take her back to Rhode Island, but she had already decided on being a Shaker. "Perhaps is was the music that convinced me to become a Shaker," Sister Mildred said many years later. "Perhaps it was the music that convinced me to become a Shaker," she said.

Her love of Shaker music was passionate, involved, and extraordinary. Like a sponge, she mentally absorbed hundreds of songs the old-fashioned way, orally, in the Shaker tradition. Her capacity to remember not only the words and music, but also knowledge of the special occasions when one or the other might be sung, was remarkable. She is solely credited with rescuing Shaker hymnody, reviving it with her contagious enthusiasm ensuring its survival. When an opportunity arose for her to give back to "the world" what she had been given, she eagerly collaborated with Daniel Patterson in his monumental 1979 *The Shaker Spiritual*, the quintessential study of Shaker hymnody.

Sisters Frances and Mildred (l-r) with Brother Arnold. Copyright Judith Adams

Sister Mildred was also a vital force in efforts to preserve Shaker books and manuscripts. She carefully maintained the collection at Alfred, which she considered sacred records of the church and its history. When the Alfred community closed in 1931 and consolidated with Chosen Land, fifty miles to the north, she incorporated the two communities' literary holdings into one where the whole was "sacredly kept."

Sister Mildred worked in the jelly, jam, and candy-making business shortly after her arrival at Chosen Land. She successfully oversaw this industry until 1968. A powerful personality with a brilliant mind and a charisma to match, she rose in leadership and was selected Trustee in 1950, giving her control over all of the community's business and financial matters. She later emerged in 1971 as the community's spiritual leader, as well. It was a turbulent time for the Shaker church, and it was about to get worse. But she found a kindred spirit in a young man from Massachusetts, Theodore Johnson, who joined forces with her to ensure the survival of her beloved Shaker faith.

Sister Mildred died in 1990 following a brief battle with cancer. She had been a Shaker for more than 85 years. She was "the greatest Shaker who ever lived," according to Sister Frances Carr, the current spiritual leader of America's Shakers, and a beloved friend.

Brother Theodore E. Johnson 1930–1986

Brother Ted standing in front of the Meeting House, 1980.

Theodore E. Johnson was born in Boston, Massachusetts. He discovered Shakerism in October 1957 on a visit to Hancock Shaker Village, where elderly Believers there urged him to contact the more vibrant Shaker community in Maine, which he did. Soon after he found work as a librarian in Maine at the Waterville Public Library.

His early education prepared him well for the work he undertook. He received his undergraduate degree in Classics from the prestigious Colby College in Maine. A Fulbright scholar, he later received a graduate degree in theology from Harvard Divinity. Had he not found the Shakers, he said, he might have joined an Episcopal monastic order.

Theodore Johnson did find the Shakers, though, and he began spending a great deal of time with them at Chosen Land. He started living there in 1960 when he was given the job of Director of the Shaker Library and Museum. He signed the Covenant becoming a Shaker in 1962, and his contributions are considered revolutionary. At Chosen Land, with Sister Mildred by his side, Brother Ted did what Mother Ann did nearly 200 years prior. He "turned the world upside down," only this time it was the world of the Shakers themselves.

The Shaker leadership at Canterbury Village in New Hampshire, made the bold move to close the church, declaring there would be no new Shakers. They even chose not to recognize Brother Ted, as he came to be called,

Brother Ted working in his office in the Family's private library in the Dwelling House

as a true Shaker. Determined and undeterred, he and Sister Mildred rebelled against their Canterbury leaders by fighting back, declaring the church at Chosen Land would remain open to new converts, citing what they felt was a higher authority, the Shaker Covenant of 1830. That document, the Shaker equivalent of the U.S. Constitution, states "the door must be kept open for the admission of new members into the Church." The controversy peaked when the doors of the Meeting House at Chosen Land, closed to the public for decades, were thrown wide open by Brother Ted and Sister Mildred. They, along with their little band of Believers in Maine, welcomed "the world" to join them in worship. A line in the sand had been drawn, touching off the first and only schism in the history of the American Shaker experience. It was divisive and bitter. Battles that lasted years were won and lost on both sides, but victory eventually went to the Maine Shakers at Chosen Land under the guidance of Brother Ted and Sister Mildred.

"They had the vision that there should be a continuing active Shaker community," said Sister June, "and that Shakerism should continue as a vital force in the world, and that the Covenant should not be closed. That we should continue to spread the message of Shakerism."

Another significant accomplishment of Brother Ted was his successful establishment of a world-class research facility and library at Chosen Land. His efforts ensure that scholars, students, and all people who simply love "all things Shaker" will have access to the faith's literary legacy for years to come. In addition, he founded and edited the Shaker Quarterly.

Thanks to Brother Ted and Sister Mildred, the faith the world found within the Meeting House at Chosen Land after the 1960s was a new Shaker faith. It honored rather than subverted or discarded decades of spiritual seeking by Brothers and Sisters who had gone before. Grounded in and emboldened by his broad-based theological understanding, Brother Ted was able to present the faith in a way that illuminated its unique contribution to the universal

Brother Ted and Sister Mildred stand united at the 1984 "Friends of the Shakers" annual summer meeting at Chosen Land.

The Meeting House seems especially
inviting across a field of flowers.
© Brian Vanden Brink.

"ongoing conversation" between God and mankind. He renewed Shakerism
not by reaching outside of it or ignoring parts of it, but by immersing himself in it and articulating its message for today with graceful authority.

Brother Ted died unexpectedly in 1986. Ironically, the Shaker Library
he worked so many years to establish was completed with donations made
in his memory. His most significant contribution, however, may have been
his efforts to bring converts to the faith. He is credited with bringing Brother
Arnold and Brother Wayne into the fold at Chosen Land.

Shakers

Seekers, true: but they could be me or you

...don't worry about how to defend yourself or what to say, for the Holy Spirit will teach you at that time what needs to be said.

LUKE 12:11–12

"The Family," October 2003. An informal portrait in the dining room of the Dwelling House following their noon meal. l-r: Sisters June and Frances and Brothers Wayne and Arnold

The Road to Chosen Land

I doubt it was a coincidence that I came to know the Shakers. I just don't believe in coincidences any longer. What I do believe is that something bigger and more powerful than anything I could ever imagine, an invisible "tide" if you will, drew me away from my Ohio home and pulled me closer and closer to Chosen Land until I found myself among the Shakers.

It was early summer, 1992. I had come to Maine four months earlier with my husband and infant twin sons to take a news anchor job in Portland. When my parents, devout Catholics who never missed Sunday Mass, were coming to visit, I figured it would be nearly impossible to find them a local Catholic church. I live in a rural part of Maine where there are no

A little-used dirt road cutting through the Maine woods is but one of many paths leading to Chosen Land.

A view of Chosen Land from the south along old State Route 26 in New Gloucester, Maine.

sidewalks or strip malls, and some of the homes are literally off the grid, but I had to try.

Within minutes of finalizing my parents' travel plans, I was in the company of a neighbor asking if she knew of a Catholic church nearby. "There's one about twenty miles away, in the next town over," she said. "But if you're looking for something closer, there's a wonderful little non-denominational church a mile up that dirt road over there." She pointed toward a heavily wooded area where there were no homes, only mature hardwoods and towering white pines.

Indeed, about fifty yards in front of me, where the town line changes from Raymond to New Gloucester, was the end of a paved road built by a modern community and the beginning of a dirt road originally carved out of the thick Maine woods by people from a different era. The dichotomy struck me even then as some kind of sign preparing me for the coming tide.

"What's the name of that road?" I asked.

"Shaker Woods Road," she said. "It belongs to the Shakers. There's a group of them living up there on the hill in a big red brick house. You can't miss it. Their church is right across the street and it's open to the public. Sunday service is at ten o'clock sharp. They don't like it if you're late."

Even before she finished her sentence, I knew I would go there—though I knew very little about the Shakers and nothing about their faith.

That Sunday's Meeting was a spiritual turning point for me. The Shakers fascinated me (there were six back then), and I was captivated by their peculiar, yet totally appealing faith. I did not take my parents to Chosen Land because the talk of a "Father/Mother" God would surely have caused one, if not both, of them to go into cardiac arrest. The Shaker church, however, would quickly become my church, and I became one of the "regulars" who joined the Shakers nearly every Sunday for worship.

Regular attendance was my introduction to the Shakers themselves. When Meeting is over, everyone is invited to join the Shakers in their huge dining

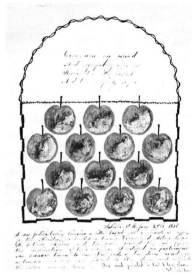

"A Little Basket Full of Beautiful Apples" by Hannah Cohoon, 1856.

The writing reads:
>   Come, come my beloved
>   And sympathize with me
>   Receive the little basket
>   And the blessing so free

I saw Judith Collins bringing a little basket full of beautiful apples for the Ministry, from Brother Calvin Harlow and Mother Sarah Harrison. It is their blessing and the chain around the bail represents the combination of their blessing. Seen and painted in the city of Peace. By Hannah Cohoon.

Courtesy of Hancock Shaker Village, Pittsfield, Massachusetts

room for fellowship, coffee, and donuts. The conversation is always personal, and there is typically a lot of laughter. "How are the twins, Jeannine?" "Just fine, Sister June." One time I said, "Brother Wayne, I need a tractor. Should I get a John Deere or a Kubota?" To which he pronounced to the entire room, "Are you kidding!" he said, adding, "Nothing runs like a Deere!"

I even asked Sister Frances what Martha Stewart was really like when she came to Chosen Land to film a segment on Shaker cooking for her popular *Martha Stewart Living* TV show. "She was absolutely charming," said Sister Frances with the conviction of a woman whose personality is equally as strong as that of Ms. Stewart's, adding, "I don't understand why people say such mean things about her." And that was the end of that.

I got to know the Shakers quite well. I saw them laugh at each other's jokes and cry at family funerals. I was with them during times of good health and

Sun flashes across the doors to the Meeting House.

Brothers Wayne (l) and Arnold during Sunday Meeting.

when they were sick or injured. Brother Arnold was accidentally rammed by one of their enormous Scottish Highland cows, shattering one of his ribs. The accident could have killed him and he was quite shaken up about it for days. He wrote me a long e-mail when he got home from the emergency room explaining every detail of the incident. "I think she got me twice [with her horn] before I got out of range," he wrote, and "Michael drove me to the hospital, where I seemed to be a bit of a novelty. Farm accidents are no longer common, you know." I teased him about the e-mail later, saying, "They must have given you some powerful pain pills, because you never would have written me such a long, detailed e-mail. I'm a reporter, you know, and I love details!" His eyes got wide, a big grin appeared on his face, and we both enjoyed a good old-fashioned belly laugh.

On a more serious note, the Shakers stood by and supported me during a painful and protracted divorce after twenty years of marriage. Sister Frances advised me to get a good attorney, and to "keep your eye on the money, dear, because I know a lot of women who were taken advantage of by their ex-husbands." And I supported them when they needed help, either in their home, their shop, or their fields.

I'll never forget the time I was reproved by Sister Frances for not pulling my weight during Meeting. "Dear, you haven't testified for quite some time," she said. "It's important that you work at your faith when you come here. This isn't a show." I was hurt because I adored her and I had disappointed her, and I was ashamed because she was right. I had become spiritually lazy. I shared my injured feelings with another "regular," who explained to me that, as Eldress, it was Sister's job to make sure everyone participated to the best of their ability during Meeting. I was also told that Sister Frances was actually quite fond of me, something I always believed to be true, but it was good to hear it, just the same. Since then, I have received lovely, handwritten notes from Sister Frances acknowledging her love for me, and I feel the same emotion toward her.

One of the Shakers's herd of Scottish Highland bulls.

I share these private details not to brag or gossip, but rather to demonstrate my authority to tell the story of these people at a critical time in their history. I approached it not only as an experienced journalist, but also as someone who has known the Shakers for many years; a trusted friend, a neighbor, and a member of their church family. I want the world to see these people as they truly are, to learn what makes them tick, to understand the forces or circumstances that brought them to Chosen Land, and, most importantly, to understand why they stay…or go.

The bottom line is this: all four Shakers portrayed in this book are real people. They wake up in the morning and get dressed, drink coffee, do chores, walk the dog, go to work, argue over silly things, swear occasionally, talk about their health problems, hurt each other's feelings sometimes,

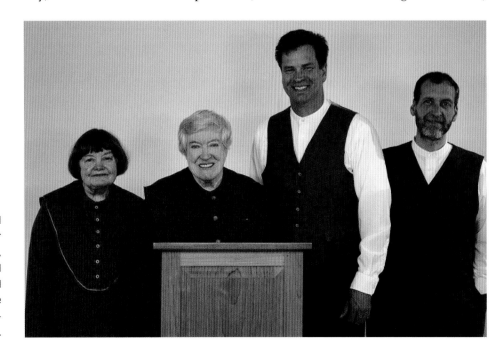

A Shaker family portrait at Chosen Land in October 2003. Left to right, Sister June, Sister Frances, Brother Wayne, and Brother Arnold. Wearing traditional Shaker dress, they stand together behind the podium in the Winter Chapel of the Dwelling House, their easy smiles radiating Shaker unity.

watch TV, and shop online—just like the rest of us. They should not be put upon pedestals simply because they are Shakers. They are not more special or even more spiritual than millions of other people who are also equally committed to their beliefs, although the Shaker's communal/celibate lifestyle is unquestionably unique.

The purpose of this book, in keeping with the spirit of Shakerism, is simple. It is not to demonstrate how different the living Shakers are from everyone else, rather, it is intended to show readers of all faiths, even those of none, how much common ground we share with them.

That said, there is one thing that only a handful of people, myself included, share exclusively with this dwindling group that constitutes what is known today as the world's smallest religion. We all felt the undeniable pull of an invisible, mighty tide that set each of us on the road to Chosen Land, and we all responded to the call without question or struggle, determined to figure out why.

Sister Francis Carr
Coming to Chosen Land in the 1930s

"I was born in Lewiston, Maine, the sixth child in my family. I had an intense religious background. My father was Baptist and I was Baptist for the first few years of my life. The 'mixed marriage' was not a good thing. My father was gone by the time I was two. By the time I was seven I had become Catholic, attended a parochial school, and had made my First Communion.

"By the time I was ten, I was pretty much an orphan. My mother was very ill and could no longer care for us. I was placed here, with the Shakers at Sabbathday Lake. At that time, they were involved in a great work of charity, taking care of children from broken homes (a common practice at all the Shaker

Elementary school photograph of Frances Carr, shortly after she began living with the Shakers at Chosen Land. Shakers commonly adopted children whose parents died or were unable to care for them. The practice resulted in a number of children choosing to join the faith when they reached 21—the age of consent. Adoption became less frequent after WWI as government social programs began to eliminate the need for orphanages. The last Shaker adoption occurred in Maine in the 1960s.

Villages that continued until the 1950s). My mother chose the Shakers because my older brother and sister were living here when I came. I think she thought as long as you can hang on to one or two that things would get better, but they did not.

"I hated it. I was so unhappy being here because having an ill mother, I had more responsibility than a normal ten-year-old child might. And I was very protective of my little sister, who came here with me. She had just turned eight. I resented that I'd become one of nine other little girls. I resented that we did things by rote. I especially resented that [caring for] my sister had been taken over by another person. I think [my anger] was probably just my way of grieving for the loss of everything that I had known up to that point.

"After I had a few days to get accustomed to my new life, I began to take on little duties. Every child had to learn to knit. Every child had to do all of the things that most rural children did. Our first chores were things like sweeping the stairs or helping in the kitchen and dining room. I did not like sewing. The only thing I liked was weaving poplar for the poplar boxes.

"Over the next two or three years some of the children went back to their parents. Sometimes it was a marital problem that was settled, and sometimes it was financial. It wasn't long after the Great Depression. They weren't great years. But for those of us who didn't have parents or a home to go back to, we became wards of the Shakers. They were responsible for us until we came of age.

"I think I was a little difficult because my brother and sister were already here and I had come once or twice to visit them. I had met Sister Jenny, she was a lovely person and a Trustee who lived at the Trustees' Office. She had nothing to do with the bringing up of children, but my mind was set on having her [take care of me], so when I came I automatically rejected the Sister

In her book *Growing Up Shaker,* Sister Frances writes, "Those who knew me as a child and as a young teenager, would never in their wildest dreams have expected that out of the ten, I would be the one to remain with the community."

Every morning, upon entering the kitchen where she has worked since she was young, Sister Frances dons an apron and prepares breakfast for the family. Here, she glances away from the bacon she is frying to explain how living the Shaker life gave her the opportunity to "be herself" as a cook, a vocation she has always found fulfilling.

in charge of the children. I feel justified in this because five years after I came here she [the Sister] left the community.

"It was not until I came to live in the Dwelling House that I found a dear friend in Eldress Prudence Stickney. There were two distinct 'orders,' a Children's Order, where we all began, and then there were teenagers, who lived in the Dwelling House. Sister Prudence was the head of the whole community. She liked my older brother a lot and I think she transferred those feelings to me. She was very astute and even though I tried to cover up my feelings [about the Sister], she saw through them. She knew I wasn't getting along with the other Sister and she allowed me to come into the Dwelling House before I was a teenager. So when I was twelve years old, I came to live in the Dwelling

House and Sister Mildred Barker became my mother from that time on. I felt an immediate rapport with her and I began to find a great deal of love and care. I was very, very happy.

Turning Point

"Sister Mildred was such a wonderful Shaker. I truly feel she was the best Shaker of that generation. She had complete love for Mother Ann, and for everything that had to do with Shakerism. She showed me a lot of special attention, which is probably what I needed. Her understanding and love made such a difference in my life.

"I remember one night she came to me just before bedtime and asked if I had said my prayers. When I told her I had not she said, 'Well, would you like to say them with me?' So we said our prayers together, and that continued every night of my life until she passed away (in 1990.) She was just that dear.

Sister Frances is the author of two books. *Growing Up Shaker* (1995) is her autobiography. *Shaker Your Plate* (1985) is a cookbook titled for a Shaker expression meant as a reminder not to waste food.

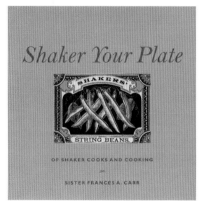

"A lot of people have asked me if I became a Shaker because of Sister Mildred, but she would never have allowed that to happen. You do not become a Shaker because of someone you like. You have to want the Shaker life and all that it involves.

"I daresay, though, that she was very influential in my decision. She told me more than once as a teenager that she worried about me. I was a ringleader, always making mischief and stirring things up. She said if I didn't settle down I might not be able to stay. That sobered me up because I didn't want to leave. I wanted to be here, even though it seemed as if I didn't. So I straightened up and I began to behave myself. I became a better kid. But nay, I would not have become a Shaker just for her."

Sister Frances working at her typewriter circa 1960.

On Choosing the Faith in 1948

"Late in the day Sister Mildred would talk to me about Shakerism. She knew I was beginning to mature and she asked me if I realized what I would be giving up and what I would be gaining if I decided to become a Shaker.

"I realized that if I became a Shaker I would never be married, I would never have children—and I love children dearly—I would be giving up all of these things. And then she explained to me what she felt she had gained by becoming a Shaker.

"[She said] Shaker life allows you to be yourself. It gives you a chance to develop whatever talents you might have. For me it was cooking.

And then there are also the religious values. I had come from a fairly strict religious home and there was one time that I even thought about becoming a nun. So, the thought of becoming a Shaker began to hold a great deal of importance for me. I became more prayerful. I became closer to Mother Ann, and I become closer, I hope, to God. By the time I was old enough to sign the Covenant and become a certified Shaker I was ready for it, I really was."

On Being an Author

"I wrote *Growing Up Shaker* (1995) because the ten girls with whom I had grown up all left the community, and during those years a lot of things took place and people said to me, 'You know, you're getting older, and you're the only one who can remember some of these things. You should probably write them down.'

"I remember President Hoover came to visit the community. He had left office, but it was still quite exciting. He and Eldress Prudence corresponded and I knew that should be recorded. I was also the only one left who had witnessed a spiritual manifestation (the actual ecstatic shaking of a Believer during worship). I knew that had to be recorded. And then, one person asked me, 'Did you write the book as therapy?' That never occurred to me, but maybe it

Sister Frances speaking to a group of Shaker Heights, Ohio schoolgirls in 1974 while speaking at a conference recognizing the bi-centennial of the Shakers' arrival in America (August 6, 1774).

was therapeutic to write about my early experiences. I've had a lot of requests to continue telling what happened.

"The cookbook (*Shaker Your Plate, 1985*) came about because so many people wanted recipes, but I found that I couldn't write about a recipe without telling about the people I had worked with as cooks. The title is from Brother Delmer Wilson (1873–1961). He always thought everyone ate too much. He sat at the head of the Brothers' table, where he had a full view of the dining room, and if he saw anyone leaving food on their plate he would come out with his gruff 'Shaker your plate.' He was referring, of course, to not wasting food. You know, the Shakers had to work hard for everything, especially when they had twenty or thirty young people to care for. You don't waste anything God gives you. Everything God gives us is a blessing, a gift. So we try not to waste anything that comes from God."

On Worldly Issues

"We give a lot of talks to schoolchildren, and one of the questions they ask quite often is 'Do you believe in abortion?' As a Shaker, I have to say I don't. If I were a woman of the world I might have very different feelings about it. We cannot believe in anything that takes life, because that goes against "Thou shalt not kill." I don't believe in capital punishment for the same reason.

"I think television is horrible, the way they constantly tout the things you *must* have. I have an eleven-year-old nephew who is the love of my life and it bothers me that he wants everything he sees. I just don't understand the way the world is. (So many) people today have not found peace, have not found happiness, and do not know God's love. They are reaching out all the time for more and more. Something's wrong. Something is lacking in their lives. I think this is why they turn to sex, drugs, and alcohol. I can't help but feel spirituality is [what's] lacking.

Brother Arnold glances through the door of the 1794 Meeting House, eyes filled with light, perhaps in expectation that the spirit will be at work in the Sunday Meeting to come.

On Thoughts of Leaving Chosen Land

"I now feel that people who grew up at Chosen Land who made the decision to become a Shaker should have lived in the world for a year [before making that decision.] When children came here to live they didn't know what the world was really like because the only time they ever left the community was to go to the doctor or dentist. The world was very alluring to them, it was all aglitter. I saw many young people leave.

"I wonder if perhaps the Shakers should have allowed people to come back. But at that time, there were a lot of people here, and the Elders probably didn't look ahead to when Chosen Land would not be filled with people of all ages.

"A lot of those who left admitted to me that the world wasn't what they thought it would be. They hadn't known what to expect, and I think many of them would have come back. They did allow some people to come back. But it should have been made clear that if you don't find happiness, and you wish you had not left, feel free to let us know.

"Maybe I should have left, like all of them, and had a year in the world. I'm sure I would have come right back because this is what I truly wanted."

Brother Arnold Hadd
Coming to Chosen Land in the 1970s

"I have been a Shaker for the last twenty-nine years. My family consists of my father and mother, and I have a younger brother and sister. I went through high school. My family were Methodists, so I was raised a Methodist.

"I didn't come here to be a Shaker, I just wanted to see what Shakerism was like in the 20th century. My first visit kind of overwhelmed me, but it

Brother Arnold relaxes in the music room of the Dwelling House after the noon meal. He loves the Shaker life, but admits it is a difficult journey for most people. "Very few people who have tried it for a year in the time I've lived here have been here at the end of a year," he points out.

didn't mean I wanted to be a Shaker. I just fell in love with the place and the people, and I very much enjoyed the worship.

"Of my many faults, being headstrong is probably the worst, and it's still very evident. When I'm right, I'm right, and that's it. It was even more so when I was sixteen. My father's family knew the Shakers in Enfield, Connecticut, just two towns away from where I grew up. A member of that community (Brother Ricardo Belden, 1870–1958) had left for a number of years. He was living with another former member in a house next door to my grandparents. My grandmother adored him. About that time Brother Ricardo went back to the Shakers, and there he remained the rest of his life until he died in the late 1950s.

"When my family went to Hancock [Shaker Village in Massachusetts] for a tour, the guide told us Brother Ricardo had been a lifelong Shaker. Afterward, I told her I enjoyed the tour, but that she was wrong, that I knew Brother Ricardo had lived and died there, but that he had been 'out' for a number of years. She told me I didn't know what I was talking about, that I was just a kid. I was so upset I went home and tried to figure out how I could prove I was right. I knew there were Shakers at Sabbathday Lake, so I wrote to them and I said that all I wanted to know was when Brother Ricardo was born, when he left, when he went back, and that I would go to Hancock and show it to them.

"Much to my surprise I got a detailed letter from Brother Ted (Brother Theodore E. Johnson, 1931–1986). The first Shaker Brother Ted ever met was Brother Ricardo, and that meeting transformed his life. Because of that I became much more intrigued with the Shakers. So I started corresponding with Brother Ted.

"What I most wanted to know was how viable Shakerism was in the 20th century. I expected the Shakers to be progressive. I hoped that they weren't still living in the 19th century. I expected linoleum. I expected wallpaper. I wanted them to be part of the 20th century. And so, for me, it was wonderful.

Shaker Brother Ricardo Belden (1870–1958) is unaware how instrumental he was in setting Brother Arnold Hadd on the road to Chosen Land. Brother Ricardo is seen here in 1935 at Hancock Shaker Village near Pittsfield, Mass., making a classic Shaker oval wooden box. His other duties included repairing clocks and sewing machines.

Brother Arnold setting type on the 1896 press in the Print Shop in the basement of the Dwelling House, circa 1990.

"Being a child of the seventies, you know, community experiments were abundant. I had gotten to know a little bit about the Sufis, and I was very drawn to some kind of community, community life. Those were the kinds of things I was asking about. And Brother Ted told me everything: what they did in daily life, what they did for prayer, things about belief, how their lives were organized and lived out. Finally, after two years of correspondence, he said, 'Why don't you just come up and see what it's like for yourself?'

"So I did, in 1974, the day after Thanksgiving. I started returning as a volunteer on weekends, sometimes for whole weeks. In 1977 I had the opportunity to be here almost the entire summer. It was at that point I realized I wanted to be a Shaker."

Chosen Faith

"I think the moment I decided I really wanted to be here was on the sixth of August 1977 (the 203-year anniversary of the Shakers' arrival in America).

We had one of the most powerful meetings I had ever witnessed. There were eight Shakers and a summer family, so probably eight or nine of us besides the community. It was a small gathering. I can't really describe it in words. It's all feeling.

"It was a time when you could feel the heavens and the earth co-mingle. There was a very real presence in the Meeting House. There was a knowledge of the presence of a myriad of Believers, and they were all there. You could feel it. Nobody said anything particularly profound, but the effect, just the outpouring of testimony from the various members, the songs, and everything else that happens, it was just . . . it was just right. It was heartfelt. It was very real.

"Brother Ted knew it before I did. We started having the kinds of conversations we hadn't had before. They came more often and lasted longer. Over the next two weeks it became apparent to Brother Ted that that's what I would do. And just before I had to go back to Massachusetts, I asked about staying at Chosen Land. The community said I could try it whenever I came back."

Chosen Land was a place where Brother Wayne felt he could approach religion through faith, and not what he perceived as through the "superstitions of other religions."

Brother Wayne Smith
Growing Up with Spiritual Tension

"I'm forty years old. I came here twenty years ago and have spent my entire adult life at the community.

"I was raised in a Baptist church. It was very evangelical so everything was 'God said it, so it must be so, and that settles it.' Being fascinated by science and the like, there were a lot of issues there.

"As a teenager, like most teens, I really started to challenge. Some of it was probably teenage rebellion, but I also think I was finding out that the things we were taught in church and what we experienced in life were at times incompatible. It created a lot of tension in my life.

"With the Shakers there was never a problem with the compatibility of God with, let's say, science or history, or anything like that. What I really like about Shakerism is that it allows for the exploration of other things, opinions, and ideas, and they're not a threat. The Shaker church doesn't see scientific advance as a threat. Science merely unlocks the secrets of God's creation, rather than challenging Biblical authority. I was much more comfortable with that idea rather than the very rigid, almost backwards view of the Baptist church I was raised in."

Coming to Chosen Land

"I was introduced to the community through Brother Theodore Johnson. He was the Latin teacher at my high school in Gray. He connected well with young people, and I talked with him. I found him to be an interesting adult. He was a very kind person. We didn't discuss anything about religion for a long time.

Young Brother Wayne in the kitchen of the Dwelling House, circa 1986.

"On one occasion Brother Arnold was going away for the weekend and they needed someone with a strong back and a weak mind to take care of the animals, and I fit the bill! I enjoyed it so much that I came back. And, you know, Brother Ted and I started talking from there. We had a lot of religious discussions after I began visiting the community. I observed things or heard things just coming here, and later I asked him about them to get an explanation. I think the greatest gift Brother Ted left me was the idea of approaching religion through faith rather than superstition.

"The thing I most enjoyed was the sense of family. No one here was related, yet it was a 'big family' kind of thing. And I enjoyed the worship services, which were very different. It was just the whole spirit of the place.

"By the time I finished high school I had so much interest in the community that I wasn't looking to go on to college or anything."

Chosen Faith: A Quiet Conversion

"There really wasn't one earth-shattering moment when I realized I wanted to be a part of the community. It was a more gradual thing. I found myself getting more and more involved, and more caught up with what was going on here. And, just being a part of things, I naturally grew into it.

"I think other people realized where my feelings were long before I did. My family and friends would ask, 'Going to the Shakers this week? It's vacation week.' And I would say, 'Yeah, I think I'm going to spend the week up there.' My desire was to be with the community, and people saw that."

Young Brother Wayne tending sheep at Chosen Land, circa 1990.

A beam of morning light falls upon a haystack in the Great Ox Barn, a Holland "square bailer" is on the right.

The Novitiate Period

"When you come to the community to live, there's a probationary period called a 'novitiate,' that generally lasts a year. It's a time for people to learn about what will be expected of them, and also for the community to learn about the individual. While we say it's a year, the novitiate period is flexible. It can be very brief. The ax can drop at any time, and that can be from either side. Someone might decide, 'maybe this isn't for me,' or the community might decide that the candidate is not going to work out. We've extended people's novitiate periods up to a year and a half before. We try to be flexible with each individual.

"By the time I completed my novitiate I'd been around the community for so long that it was really just another day. It wasn't anything special except that we had a special meal, and it was noted in the daily journal that the day marked my first formal year with the community. We mark our anniversaries every year and celebrate them as a kind of second birthday. Mine, of course, is easy to remember—it's December 7. Brother Arnold always calls it "The Day of Infamy!"

On Celibacy

Brother Wayne struggles repeatedly with questions of celibacy. Perhaps it is the pressure of the cameras, lights, and sound equipment. Perhaps it is a foreshadowing of something else.

"We practice celibacy because it's an expression of our selflessness, kind of an ultimate expression in that we hold no personal belongings; we don't even hold exclusive relationships as community members. By not marrying, we're not bound to any one person or our immediate biological relations. Rather, we are, hopefully through our celibacy, free and able to embrace all people equally, to love all of them as our sisters and brothers in Christ.

"The model is the life of Jesus and his disciples—it's just that ultimate expression of selflessness. Realizing that's the way it's going to be in heaven, we don't have exclusive relationships but are all of one heart and one mind. Ultimately, the idea is for the Shakers to begin the kingdom of heaven here on earth.

"Being celibate is not the big burning issue in the community. It's not like it's something that's sprung on you, it's not like, "Oh yeah, no more dating girls, Wayne." It's something that we know. By the time you're ready to start the community life, you understand that and you understand why you're giving it up along with everything else. It's just one more thing you give up. And for those people who have given up the community, it's not usually the celibacy, it's just been the cumulative giving up of everything.

"Celibacy is such an important part of salvation because it's part of that giving up of yourself. It's hard to articulate, but it's just part of the package. I think when you stop and think about it and you understand, it's just…you know, you don't look at anyone any longer and say, 'That's my wife.' or 'That's my husband.' Rather, now you see people as your brother and your sister."

On Salvation

"A lot of people think, 'Well, the Shakers think everyone has to be celibate to find salvation.' But I think there are many people who live ordinary lives, but because they are selfless in their lives, will still find salvation. I also think people are not damned if they do not live in a Shaker community.

Brother Wayne is without question the Family's "workhorse," the frayed and tattered sleeves of his Carhart jacket a testament to the countless hours he's spent engaged in physical labor over a span of twenty years. Those who know him well say he works equally hard to "grow" his knowledge of the inner light.

Ultimately, you know, it's God's decision. We're just doing what we feel brings us closer to God.

Looking Back

"I think about it once in a while, but I don't think I look back too much because I wouldn't be here if I did. If you're constantly looking back you're eventually going to lose focus. It's important to remember the things that drew me here, and to know if those are the same things that keep me here."

Reflection

"I believe I have found the path that will lead me to a closer union with God. I think to stay on the right path takes a lot of humility, and a lot of wisdom. And it takes a lot of prayer for both those gifts so that you can stay on the right track, because it's very easy to confuse your own desires with what God may or may not want. I think that's how people run into trouble. I think living in community helps keep you on the right path, provided everyone else remains on it. It's a collective effort.

"The important thing is that we're happy with whatever our decisions may be, whether it's as part of the community or part of a nuclear family—you have to find your happiness there."

"My favorite saying of Mother Ann's is, 'I once served God through fear, but now I serve him through love.' I think that sums up the whole transition from Old Testament to New, because in the Old Testament there was a God of punishment and people were always erring and had to be brought back into line. In the New Testament comes the whole message of God's love. We get this idea of forgiveness, of starting over, of healing. I think in our own faith journey fear is oftentimes where we start. But you have to progress from that because I don't think you can truly understand God if you're afraid of God. You have to move from fear and awe to love."

"I am content here," says Sister June Carpenter, smiling at her work in the Library.

Sister June Carpenter
A Spiritual Child

"I'm 65 years old. I'm from Brookline, in eastern Massachusetts. I was a librarian, a cataloger in the public library.

"I wanted to be close to God even when I was a child. My parents always took me to Sunday school. The church we went to was called "Federated." It was a combination of Baptist and Congregationalist. I had a good religious background.

"My mother and I went into Boston one day and I saw a lot of people. I could see that God was within each of them. I've always remembered that— that God must be inside everyone in some way, whether they realize it or not. That was a spiritual thing I experienced, that went away after a while. You can't stay on the mountaintop all the time. Like the Shakers say, 'you have to come down into the valley,'…that's where most of life is.

"My mother was widowed when I was fifteen and I wanted to help her out as she got older, so I lived with her until she passed away in 1985."

Coming to Chosen Land in 1988

"I had a friend who brought me here. She was interested in the Shakers because she's a Christian Scientist and there are some similarities between the faiths. She had contributed to the fund to renovate the [Shaker] schoolhouse and when she was invited to the dedication she asked me to come, too.

"It was a very hot and humid day, so we didn't stay for the dedication, but we did go on the tour. I was so impressed with the place. It seemed very spiritual. I just wanted to come back and be closer to it, because ever since I was in college, when I first read about people who had religious vocations and gave their lives to God, I wanted to give my life to God.

"My friend told me that the Shakers took people on as volunteers in the summer, so I called and asked if I could volunteer and told them I was a librarian.

"They had a backlog of books and they needed someone to catalog them. Since I'd been doing that for nearly thirty years, I felt right at home doing it. So I came up, and the community took me in and made me a part of its life. I liked it so much that I asked if I could be considered for membership. They let me come up and try the life for about a year, and I've been here ever since.

"I think my coming here just when they needed a cataloger was probably part of God's plan. I don't believe in coincidences. I think He has everything planned down to the minutest detail. I think He wanted me to come here."

Chosen Faith—Chosen Family

"I decided I wanted to be a Shaker after I saw the life and found that I could do something useful. I also helped out in the community. I could drive people and run errands for them, work in the garden, and help out in the dining room.

"I think when we don't have our own natural families that we have a broader outlook. And we, as God is the God of everyone, want to be friends to everyone. God taught me to see all men as my brothers and all women as my sisters, so I try to think of people that way. We pray for people and wish the best for them.

Sister June (left) with Sister Marie Burgess at the 1992 "Friends of the Shakers" annual meeting at Chosen Land. Sister Marie, who had been a Shaker nearly all her life, passed away in 2001 at the age of 81.

If we have any negative thoughts we try to overcome them. That, I think, is the perfection that the Christ calls us to, and that we're trying to work toward...being in a Spirit of perfect love toward everyone.

"I am content here."

"Little I"

"I am the last and the least of the community at the moment, and I'm very happy in that position. If I get into a position where I'm head of something, like when I was head cataloger at the library where I used to work, I feel uncomfortable and insecure. But I can cope with being little and low. It helps with the humility that we are striving for. One of the Shaker "humility songs" that I relate to is,

> Great I, Little I
> Great I can see.
> Little I is Pretty I
> So Little I will be.

It helps us to remember that we want to be a little 'I.' What I'm trying to do here is to live my life as well as I can as a Shaker, and to do what the community needs me to do."

A Shared Shaker Vision

"There's the spirit drawing by Hannah Cahoon, the 'Tree of Life,' that I can understand more than the other spirit drawings because I had an experience like that once. Many years ago, when I was very close to God, I looked at a tree and saw it shining. The leaves seemed to glow with spiritual lightas though the life within it was actually glowing. The nearest I can get to really explaining it is to say that it looked like the Tree of Life that she depictedI can understand what she was talking about because of that.

In addition to her work in the Library, Sister June also helps Sister Frances prepare meals in the kitchen.

Hannah Cohoon (1781–1864) rendered her "Tree of Life" (1854), the most famous of all Shaker gift drawings, in ink and tempera. She coated the leaves with varnish to make them sparkle. Well educated but unschooled as an artist, this otherwise undistinguished member of the Shaker family living at Hancock Shaker Village, inspired by the Spirit, gave Shakerism its most striking and resonant symbol of unity. Her image has become synonymous with America, an icon of who we are.

Sister Hannah claims Mother Ann appeared to her in a dream and gave her the inspiration for this and other gift drawings in an effort to help explain the mystical nature of Shakerism to Believers. She inscribed these words at the bottom of the image: "I received a draft of a beautiful Tree pencil'd on a large sheet of white paper bearing ripe fruit. I saw it plainly; it looked very singular and curious to me. I have since learned that this tree grows in the 'spirit Land'. Afterwards the spirit shew'd me plainly the branches, leaves and fruit, painted or drawn upon paper. The leaves were check'd or crossed'd and the same colors you see here. I entreated Mother Ann to tell me the name of this tree: which she did Oct. 1st, 4th hour P.M. by moving the hand of a medium to write twice over 'Your Tree is the Tree of Life'."

Sister Hannah's "The Tree of Life" was pictured on a UNICEF Christmas postcard in 1974 to benefit the charitable organization. Courtesy of Hancock Shaker Village, Pittsfield, Massachusetts.

It's a gift that God gives you, to make you realize He is always there, that He loves you, and that He always cares for you. And you know, I don't worry about things. I would like to be a Shaker for the rest of my life because I think God wants me to be one."

Place
Heaven on earth

A single tree in a pasture at Chosen Land bears a slight resemblance to the one Shaker Sister Hannah Cohoon saw in a vision of heaven, then drew for the benefit of Believers.

"Thy Kingdom come. Thy will be done, on earth as it is in heaven.

MATTHEW 6:10

The Kingdom Life

Unique spiritual names, such as City of Peace, Holy Grove, and Wisdom's Valley were given to each Shaker village during the 1840s to enhance a powerful wave of spiritualistic revivalism that swept through all the Shaker communities. Chosen Land was adopted in 1848 by the Sabbathday Lake community, which at the time was the most remote, and one of the smallest and poorest of all the villages. It was so seemingly vulnerable to demise that Shakers themselves referred to its inhabitants as "the least of Mother's children in the East." How ironic for Chosen Land to have outlasted them all. And it is here, in a cluster of historic buildings surrounded by hundreds of acres of Maine farmland, that today's Shakers practice their chosen faith. They are utopian idealists, following in the footsteps of generations of radical religious thinkers, who believe the perfectibility of mankind is achievable through life in a perfect society.

Chosen Land Shaker Village in New Gloucester Maine, in 1850. Detail from a watercolor by Shaker Elder Brother Joshua H. Bussell (1816–1900) of Alfred, Maine, in the collection at the Shaker Library at Chosen Land.

Chosen Land, like all Shaker communities, was specifically designed to be a place where this perfect, faith-based "Kingdom Life" could be lived. Zion was the template, eternal salvation the prize for those who could achieve the mystical state of mind where heaven and earth are one.

To be honest, the concept of a united heaven and earth was difficult for me to understand. The notion of 'time' kept getting in the way. It's impossible, I would argue, to be in two places at once. My understanding was that you live first on earth, then, after you die, if you've been good, you go to heaven. But that's not how it works for Shakers, and it wasn't until Brother Arnold explained it to me in terms I could relate to that it made sense.

Mist rising off Sabbathday Lake combines with the pink and gold hues of a crisp October morning to create an ethereal backdrop for a small flower garden framed by the Herb House (right) and the Museum (left).

Place

This gift drawing was "received" in 1849 by Sister Polly Jane Reed of Hancock Shaker Village and is titled, "A Present from Mother Lucy to Eliza Ann Taylor." It is filled with symbols of hope such as a trumpet of wisdom, a flower of love and purity, and a message of glad tidings. Courtesy of Hancock Shaker Village, Pittsfield, Massachusetts.

"Why," he asked, "when people recite The Lord's Prayer, do they pray, 'Thy Kingdom come. Thy will be done, on earth as it is in heaven?' They should strive to live that right now—not wait for it."

"I never thought about it that way," I said tentatively, "because I thought it was taken care of for me."

"But Christ makes us responsible." he said slowly, making sure I was listening carefully. "Shakers come to an understanding that to be a Believer, that is the call to live, or attempt to live, the Kingdom Life here and now. Perhaps the greatest gift Mother Ann gave us is our understanding of how to live that life. One of our songs says,

> Here below we are forming a heaven,
> A robe that the angels are wearing.

"The concept is that you don't have to wait for something to happen. We are called as Christians to show forth Christ's Kingdom here on earth. One of the many names we've had over the years is the Millennial Church, because we believe we are living in the millennium here and now."

"That's what the Shakers are working toward, building the Kingdom (of Heaven) here in this world, and not waiting to get into it," Sister June concurred.

Sister Frances agrees. "One thing people don't understand about Shaker theology is that we are expected to do everything possible to make that Kingdom on earth a reality. I have to do all that I can to make life as much of a heaven for people on earth as possible."

"But what does that mean?" I asked, pushing for concrete examples.

"Celibacy is one of the things to make the Kingdom come to life," she said. "People say, 'Why don't you marry?' Because Jesus never married, and we are striving to build up the Kingdom here on earth."

The community's old telephone is not used for anything other than a convenient place to post "sticky" notes these days, having long ago been replaced by modern communication systems that feature multiple lines, speed dial, and call waiting.

"We also believe in Christian hospitality," she continued. "We are expected to meet everyone as though it might be the Christ. I try very hard to put that into action."

That's when I remembered an incident a few weeks earlier in her kitchen involving a family from Germany. A family of four, two adults and two small children, entered the Shakers' dining room where I was speaking with Sister Frances about an upcoming shoot. The Dwelling House, where the Shakers live, is off limits to the public, but the man asked Sister Frances in broken English (perhaps explaining why he didn't heed the "Community Members Only" sign on the door) about a tour. She was gracious beyond what words in any language would convey. She motioned for them to sit at her table, walked into the kitchen and brought back a still steaming blueberry pie she had just

Thick New England fall foliage almost, but not quite, conceals the brilliant white atop the 1883 Dwelling House. When seen from above, the steeple seems to mark Chosen Land as a home for spiritual seekers who truly believe that heavenly portals can, indeed, be found here on earth.

made for the noon meal. Sister June was only a few steps behind with plates, forks, and napkins. I remember thinking how generous it was of the Shaker sisters and I wondered if I would have been so gracious. Looking back, it was an example of seeing the Christ spirit in everyone, and today I understand the Sisters' actions on a much deeper level.

The Kingdom, I now understand, is not a "place" fixed in future time. It's an attitude, a way of life, a conscious state of mind. Humanity is capable, I believe, of creating heaven here on earth, We can do it collectively or individually, even if only in our minds, which may be the only place that counts.

Sister Frances tells a wonderful story about a similar incident of spontaneous hospitality that occurred at Chosen Land around 1900. It's about a disheveled "tramp" who showed up at the village, apparently lost and hungry after wandering in the area. One of the Sisters welcomed him, spoke with him about the village, then sent him on his way after giving him some food and drink. The "tramp" turned out to be Charles Tiffany, president of Tiffany and Company in New York City, who was staying at the nearby Poland Spring House, an exclusive resort that catered to the rich and famous of the day. Mr. Tiffany was so moved by the Shakers' hospitality that he sent them a letter of gratitude explaining who he was—along with a complete silver service for their table. That singular act of unconditional charity was a heavenly moment. It was a glimpse of the Kingdom Life. The goal for Shakers is to create as many of these moments as possible.

When I began documenting life at Chosen Land in October of 2000, there were six Shakers. By 2005, when my research was complete, membership was down to four—Sister Minnie Greene, who was being cared for in a nearby nursing home, died at age 90 in January 2001. Sister Marie Burgess died six months later at age 81.

I often wonder what will happen if/when there are no more Believers to care for the village. My guess is that should Chosen Land ever cease to be the

A rising sun reveals the Shakers' sheep wandering the rolling hills of Chosen Land. Says Brother Wayne of the beauty and bounty of their material riches, "We see it as a privilege to have these things, and we need to improve our lot and show good stewardship. They're more on loan than to keep forever."

Place

home of a living Shaker, it will most certainly become a museum, like many of the other non-active villages have; and, for those of us who will remember the difference, something will be missing. Even so, that doesn't mean the spirit of Chosen Land can't be experienced elsewhere here on earth. After all, to paraphrase Brother Arnold, the opportunity to live the Kingdom Life is something millions of Christians ask God for every day. Together, I believe, we can make it happen. Perhaps it begins by trying to see the face of Christ in everyone.

The Village
An 'open-door' policy in a world apart

Chosen Land is a prism that allows the "world's people" to look directly into the soul of Shakerism—its people and their ways. An estimated 10,000 visitors, mostly from New England, but some from around the globe, travel here in search of a deeper understanding of the Shaker experience, be it the faith, the history, the furniture, or some combination.

From a distance the village appears frozen in time, but once past the white picket fence there's no denying this special, sacred place is alive and well. The village was declared a National Historic Landmark in 1974. With its iconic American architecture and classic New England landscape, it is visually spectacular. The rolling hills speckled with flocks of meandering sheep and Scottish Highland cattle make for a shutterbug's dream, and visitors commonly arrive with cameras around their necks. Brother Wayne speaks of his Family's abundance of riches with a deep sense of responsibility and humility.

"We see our buildings, our animals, and our place in the world as a kind of stewardship," he says. "Rather than saying, 'We own this big house, we own this big barn, we own these cows, we own this land,' we see it as a privilege to

Shaker-inspired architecture has left a distinctive imprint on the American landscape, especially in New England. The peaked rooflines of three Shaker structures, as seen from a southern pasture, point in unison toward the heavens.

have these things, and we need to improve our lot and show good stewardship. They're more on loan than to keep forever."

"[We] have to remember to be hospitable, because this is God's house, not ours," explains Sister June. "He is trying to invite as many people to Him as possible, so we want to be as open as we can about having anyone come. We try to do what we can to be open, friendly, kind, and generous."

Shakers have historically shared their wealth, both natural and material, by welcoming the public into their homes, shops, libraries, museums, and houses of worship. They want to be understood for who they truly are. They want the world to understand their faith, which is typically overlooked in favor of their furniture. More importantly, they need the exposure. Because Shakers are celibate, they do not bear children who grow up in the faith in the way many people are "born" into a particular religion by their parent's beliefs. That's why the Shakers' "open-door" policy is so crucial. It is their single most important tool for attracting converts. It is precisely how Sister June and Brothers Wayne and Arnold discovered Chosen Land, and ultimately the Shaker way of life.

Sunday Meeting is the community's most important outward demonstration of Shakerism, and the public is encouraged to join them in worship. But it wasn't always that way.

"For a long time, all during my growing-up years," recalls Sister Frances, "we never had anyone who did not belong to the Shaker community attend worship service. But when Brother Ted came to live here (1960), he and Sister Mildred felt that if people really wanted to be a part of the Shaker worship service, why not? No church should be closed to anyone," said Sister Frances, echoing the sentiment of Mother Ann Lee herself.

"We're trying to take the community and make it God's chosen land here on earth where you not only hear about the gospel, but you see it being lived every day," says Brother Wayne.

"That's something we work on here, to surrender to God and try to do His will," explained Sister June. "That's part of taking up the cross. You try not to do what you want, but what God wants, and here in the community that boils down to what others want you to do."

That selfless perspective was a difficult position for the Shakers to take in 2003, when a ten-mile section of Route 26 was slated for rerouting. The narrow, highly trafficked road runs right through the middle of Chosen Land, passing within a few feet of the front porch steps of the Shakers' 1883 home, their 1794 Meeting House, and several other historic structures.

Ironically, it was Maine Shaker brethren who cut that stretch of road by hand in the early 1800s, from their village to nearby Gray. They carved out a lovely, winding path that followed the curvaceous shoreline of their beloved Sabbathday Lake. A century and a half later, however, those sharp twists and

The physical appearance of Chosen Land was dramatically transformed in 2003 by a Maine Department of Transportation road re-routing project. The Shakers, like many of their neighbors, lost land to the state through eminent domain. The original, two-lane, dangerously narrow and winding Route 26 ran through the middle of the Shakers' village, and can be seen running parallel to the white fence in the photograph. The new, multi-lane highway is straighter, wider, and much safer, but part of the Shakers' commercial apple orchard was sacrificed in the name of progress.

turns had become a death trap for motorists. In the late 1990s there was a public outcry to make the road safer through a multi-million-dollar widening and straightening project.

Additionally, Route 26 had become a major east/west thoroughfare slicing across the state, and truck traffic on the road had become so intense that vibrations were buckling the foundations of several historic Shaker buildings. Something had to be done, but people living along the road, including the Shakers, couldn't agree on where the new road should go, so the State of Maine stepped in. Department of Transportation officials developed a plan to redirect Route

26 away from the lakeshore, making it straighter, wider, and, ultimately, safer. Protest erupted, though, when the State announced it would invoke eminent domain, and take certain property, including some owned by the Shakers, to make the controversial plan work.

On one hand the Shakers were pleased when they learned the new Route 26 would be situated hundreds of yards away from their Dwelling House, virtually eliminating traffic in front of their home. But they were heartbroken when the state officials announced the new and improved highway would cut right through the heart of their beautiful 25-acre commercial apple orchard.

The State of Maine's 2003 land grab resulted in the most dynamic physical alteration to Chosen Land in the history of the village. The situation was not resolved the way the Shakers had hoped, but countless motor vehicle accidents have likely been avoided as a result. The family accepted the state's decision without protest—a surrender, perhaps, to the will of a higher power in lieu of their interests.

The village is much less noisy now that the sound of trucks and tractor-trailers carrying everything from oversized mobile homes to timber from the northern part of the state is all but a distant rumble. There is hardly any traffic on the old paved road in front of the Shakers' home, and it is much safer now that they and their thousands of annual visitors no longer have to cross the road to reach the buildings on the other side.

Time will tell whether the new serenity at Chosen Land is too high a price for a community dependent on exposure to attract converts. All that traffic over so many years put Chosen Land quite literally "on the map" for millions of people driving by.

Traveling on the new road these days it's easy to miss the village. The Shakers posted a new sign near the highway identifying the turn-off to their community, but it can still be easily overlooked.

The good news is that the Shakers' eye-catching, historic 1903 water tower, which over the years has come to symbolize Chosen Land itself, is now quite visible to passing motorists. There is much hope that this structure, originally built to store water for fire suppression at Chosen Land, will now protect and nourish the Shakers in a different way.

White picket fences run parallel in many places to the two-lane road that runs through Chosen Land. This particular fence, seen through rippled panes of antique glass in the Meeting House, casts a peculiar view of the outside world.

The cold steel backside of a 20th-century stove contrasts with the warmth of the wooden Shaker rocker & original built-in corner cupboard.

The Brick Dwelling House
Home Sweet Home

The brick Dwelling House is a massive, five-and-a-half-story, red brick structure begun in 1883. It replaced an older three-and-a-half-story dwelling house that had served for 89 years. Shaker brethren cut most of the timber for the project on Shaker land. They also discovered granite about a quarter mile away, set up a quarry operation, and cut enough blocks for the foundation of their new home. Family records indicate 230,000 bricks were used during construction that took nearly two years to complete.

It is the largest single structure at Chosen Land, as well as in the town of New Gloucester, and it consists of several bedrooms, offices, a sitting room, storerooms, a music room, and a large kitchen/dining room complex that occupies most of the ground floor. There is also a chapel on the second floor that is used for Sunday services approximately seven months a year because the Meeting House across the street is unheated.

Now that the Family is down to four, there is a cavernous feeling to the upper chambers of this imposing building where dozens of Shakers once lived and slept, sisters on one side, brothers on the other. But there are signs everywhere that a 21st-century family still lives here. From sweaters and coats hanging on pegs along the wall in the main hallway, to LL Bean boots and bowls of dog food on the floor, this is a real family's home sweet home.

The characteristic trademarks of all Shaker interiors, designed to segregate the sexes, are abundant throughout and include gender-specific staircases that rise to the attic. Other well-recognized Shaker designs such as built-in storage systems can also be seen in virtually every room.

The Dwelling House by all accounts was, and continues to be, the community's command center. It is where Believers live, eat, sleep, check in with

A single Adirondack chair on the back porch of the Dwelling House.

each other, and pray amid a plethora of museum-quality Shaker art and artifacts. The rooms currently in use are comfortable and modest, decorated with a mixed collection of authentic hand-made Shaker furniture that stands alongside mass-produced furniture from the 1890s through the 1980s.

Shakers living at Chosen Land today, unlike Shakers from past generations, frequently spend time together. It is probably the biggest change in the manner in which the home is used. Segregation of the sexes is no longer strictly enforced. Today's Shakers eat many meals sitting at the same table. They also frequently gather at the end of the day in a second-floor family room to relax, chat, and watch TV on an old set given to them by a friend. Sister Frances takes a no-nonsense approach to segregation of the sexes, saying, "It's not necessary. We all know why we're here."

The 1883 Dwelling House.

They do segregate in their home, however, for most meals, on special occasions, and when they are in the company of people from outside the community who are not among their close friends. They are always segregated during worship.

The Dwelling House is one of Chosen Land's twelve (out of eighteen) buildings that is not open to the public. That helps keep its current caretakers from feeling as though they live in a fishbowl, but that wasn't always the case. "For many years people on tour were brought into the dining room and kitchen to see what was going on," recalls Sister Frances. "That was a little troublesome for me. I mean, your kitchen can get very messy. So we finally closed that out."

A simple, unpretentious wooden sign planted firmly in the ground, like the aged and stately trees at Chosen Land, identifies the Shaker's house of worship. The centuries old Meeting House is unheated, except for woodstoves that are no longer used, and it is only used during the summer and early fall.

Brother Arnold enters the historic 1794 Meeting House at Chosen Land.

This remarkable 19th-century structure is most striking because it serves as a fascinating study in contrast. Historic and culturally significant remnants from the past are everywhere, in virtually every nook and cranny. But so, too, are telltale reminders that this is not just a sterile museum, despite its designation in 1974 as a National Historic Landmark. The Dwelling House is unquestionably home to a modern-day family, even though a few of the rooms are not like yours or mine.

The 1794 Meeting House
A Modest 'House Church' for Today

Mother Ann Lee did not like the Anglican churches of her native England. To her, they were pompous displays of worldly excess; their statues, steeples, and stained glass offended her spiritual sensibilities. Her attitude toward religious architecture and her disdain for a hierarchal clergy were likely born out of the anti-authoritarian impulse of the Protestant Reformation.

"She was a 'house church' person," Brother Arnold says, adding, "that was the intimacy; that's what helped make the dynamic of Mother work. She would meet them right in the home." And it was in these intimate spaces that Mother Ann gathered many a "kitchen convert."

When Shaker membership grew to the point where it was no longer feasible to worship in individuals' homes, they decided to gather into distinct faith-based communities where they erected architecturally unique "meetinghouses," rejecting the term "church" outright. They agreed on a style: plain, white clapboarded structures with a gambrel roof. They agreed on a "housewright," a Shaker master craftsman named Moses Johnson. He supervised the building of an astounding ten meetinghouses in ten years for New England

This photo of the 1794 Meeting House was taken in 1962 as part of the "Historic American Buildings Survey." The Meeting House has remained virtually unchanged over the with the exception of a stair wing (on the right) that was added in 1839.

A worn blue pew, burnished through to wood by the hands of generations of Believers, is a simple but eloquent reminder of the continuity of faith at Chosen Land. The original "Prussian blue" paint on the un-restored surface was made from sage blossoms, indigo, and blueberry skins mixed in milk.

Modern-day Shaker 'parishioners' gather outside the 1794 Meeting House at Chosen Land prior to joining the Shakers for Sunday Meeting. It is the last original Shaker Meeting House, out of ten designed by Shaker master craftsman Brother Moses Johnson, still in use today.

Shaker communities. The structures were unpretentious, but to the Shakers, they were the crown jewel of the village.

On April 19 and 20, 1794, the approximately one hundred Believers living at Sabbathday Lake in Maine agreed to formally organize as a community, becoming the 11th United Society of Believers in the country. They memorialized the occasion by beginning work on a meetinghouse for public worship.

The Meeting House at Chosen Land looks today almost exactly as it did in the 18th century. Its white plaster walls are offset by the sharply contrasting original "Prussian blue" painted beams and well-worn wainscoting. Inside it is wide open; the benches are unfixed, so they can be pushed up against the walls or even hung on Shaker-designed peg rails built high on the walls. What is most remarkable, architecturally, is that there are no posts to support the weight of the second floor that was used for additional living and work space. Posts would have impeded the ecstatic worship that was so common in the 18th and 19th centuries, so they had to design a structure to accommodate their needs.

Brother Moses even built little "galleries" into his meetinghouses for the world's people, especially Victorian-era tourists, who came to watch the Shakers worship. The twirling, whirling, and shaking of the Believers under the influence of the Spirit was a great source of fascination and entertainment throughout the 1800s. The tourists often purchased souvenirs from the Shakers' gift shop, such as oval wooden boxes and hand-woven baskets. These so-called "fancy goods" made by Shaker Brothers and Sisters make up a large part of the artifacts that command such spectacular prices at auction today.

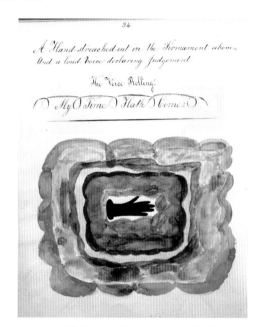

These days the atmosphere during meeting is different. People expecting religious theater will be disappointed, says Sister Frances. "I feel there are times when people come here to be entertained. I won't say that has never happened. We have had people come who have been a little troublesome. But on the whole, people come here because they want to join the service." And on any given Sunday when the weather is warm, that is what you will see—dozens of spiritual seekers, mostly locals and "summer people" joining the Shakers in worship, song, and praise in a "house church" inspired by Mother Ann.

Gift drawing from page 34 of the "Book of prophetic signs written by Prophet Isaiah" in 1843, by Sister Miranda Barber. Ink, watercolor, and graphite on paper, leather-bound. 8 ½ x 6 ¹³⁄₁₆ inches. Courtesy of The Western Reserve Historical Society, Cleveland, Ohio.

The Meeting House is often referred to by non-Shakers who worship there as an important part of their attraction to Shakerism. They are likely unaware that their preference for simple, unadorned, intimate houses of worship is a key indicator for identifying members of the rapidly emerging Postmodern Christian church, many of whom are increasingly rejecting the megachurches of the 1980s and 90s in favor of smaller gatherings in less pretentious structures.

The Shakers' historic preference for simple, unconventional houses of worship is yet another striking similarity to a burgeoning "new age" of Christianity that is literally sweeping the planet.

The Library
'Ark of the Covenant'

The written word has always been of utmost importance to the Shakers, and they were prolific writers. The Shakers, beginning in 1790, used printing and publishing to help explain their unique way of life to the world. It is a tradition carried on today by Brother Arnold, who is an accomplished pressman and enjoys working in the Print Shop.

The world-class Shaker research facility at Chosen Land attracts scholars, students and visitors from around the world. The Library is housed in the Shakers' 1880 one-room schoolhouse that underwent a monumental restoration project in 1986. © JERRRY AND MARCY MONKMAN/ECOPHOTOGRAPHY

Lock and key on worn cupboard door in the Library.

The vision to build a library at Chosen Land began in the early 1880s with Elder Otis Sawyer. He wanted to preserve important Shaker writings and, by 1882, had gathered 191 items written by or about Shakers. He stored the writings in the Ministry's Shop in a beautiful Shaker-made bookcase crafted of butternut wood. He wrote, "This collection is intended to comprise not only all religious works, but some catalogues of garden seeds, herbs, and other articles of manufacture and merchandise which will present to posterity the enterprise and industrial pursuits of our worthy ancestors."

A century later the butternut bookcase is still in use, but today it stands even taller in a home of its own—the Sabbathday Lake Shaker Library, dedicated in 1988. It is a world-class repository of information on Shaker heritage and faith comprised of more than 100,000 individual items. Books, rare manuscripts, periodicals, maps, scrapbooks, ephemera, microfilm, and an audio/video collection are all available to the public by appointment year-round.

Credit for establishing the permanent library, one capable of archiving a collection as rare and important as one that documents the history of the American Shaker movement, belongs to Brother Ted. He set the wheels in motion to renovate the Shakers' 1880 schoolhouse that had been sold in 1957 and actually moved off the property. He repurchased the schoolhouse, laid a new foundation, and began the process for turning the dilapidated structure into a museum-quality, state-of-the-art research facility, complete with a two-level fireproof vault.

Sadly, Brother Ted never realized his dream. He died unexpectedly in 1986 at the age of 55, two years before the dedication ceremony. It was his death, ironically, that provided the funds to finish the monumental job. His untimely passing prompted an outpouring of donations that were used "to move all of our priceless manuscripts, photographs, and printed works in our collections over to a fireproof, climate-controlled situation where they can be preserved for all time," said Brother Arnold, the community's historian.

Sister June is a voracious reader who enjoys being surrounded by books. Her former career as a librarian leaves her well suited as one of the caretakers of the Shakers' prized library.

The significance of the library, especially to the Shakers themselves, is hard to overstate. The 1882 words of Elder Otis Sawyer perhaps say it best: "This repository may be considered the sacred Archive or Ark of the Covenant like the one in the ancient temple of Solomon which held the sacred treasures and documents."

Tourists, such as this group seen in sun-drenched silhouette through an open barn door, are encouraged to explore the multiple buildings that comprise the Museum "experience." What distinguishes Chosen Land from other Shaker museums and villages is that it remains the only active community in existence.

The Museum
To Tell the Truth

The Museum at Chosen Land serves a purpose similar to that of the Library. It was established in 1926 by Sister Iona Sedgley with the goal of educating the public about the "truths" of Shakerism. Since then, hundreds of thousands of visitors have enjoyed the opportunity to experience a slice of Shaker life, past and present.

The Museum, open Memorial Day through Columbus Day (excluding Sundays), is actually a collection of six buildings at Chosen Land that the public is welcome to explore with the assistance of a guide. Inside the buildings are 27 exhibit rooms covering more than 200 years of Shaker history, with emphasis on the Maine Shaker experience.

The Museum's permanent exhibits house the largest repository of Maine Shaker culture. Fine examples of furniture, woodenware, oval boxes, tin and metal wares, tools and technology, "fancy" sales goods, textiles and costumes, visual arts, as well as medicinal and herbal products are among the 13,000 artifacts currently housed in the Sabbathday Lake collection.

The Trust for Public Land
Shakers, not Movers

A financial storm was on the horizon for the Shakers in 2001. Rising property taxes and reduced revenues threatened the Shakers' ability to keep their hilltop village intact. Although much attention is paid to the historic value of the architecture at Chosen Land, little is typically given to the priceless nature of the land itself. The health of the region's watershed depends on the health of the Shakers' land, the largest undivided parcel of property in the watershed. The Shakers' forests and wetlands, including a 150-acre bog, are crucial to maintaining the ecological health of the watershed. Everything was at risk, the land, the buildings, and the village itself, if the Shakers couldn't pay their taxes.

The problem began right at home. New Gloucester and Poland, the two towns in which the Shakers' land sits, were quickly becoming bedroom communities of Portland, Maine's largest city, only about twenty minutes away by car. Pressure to sell and develop land in those two towns was driving up taxes. Unlike most religious organizations, Shakers always paid their taxes. They paid $27,000 in property taxes alone in 2005. A hike would be devastating. So, after much prayer and research, the family began investigating alternative ways to preserve and protect their significant land holdings. They turned to a variety of conservation and preservation groups in an effort to devise a plan that would prevent any chance of their land falling victim to urban sprawl. After several years of negotiating, fundraising, and a tremendous amount of hard work on the part of the Shakers, along with help from some of the most respected organizations in the country, they formed a perpetual charitable organization to safeguard their historic landscape.

The 1,700 acres of mostly forested Chosen Land, now under the protection of powerful conservation easements, will be preserved for generations to come.
© JERRY AND MARCY MONKMAN/ECOPHOTOGRAPHY

Sabbathday Lake

Upon thy shores, O lovely lake,
   This calm, mid-summer day,
I seem to hear a voice which tells
   Of ages passed away.

That, long before the birth of men,
   Through many waiting years,
You saw the forest rise, and heard
   The music of the Spheres.

And then the Indian came, from whence,
   The mystery is sealed.
We question history, old and new,
   It has not been revealed.

But this we know, he trod these shores,
   His fields of maize here grew;
You saw the wigwam in the shade,
   You bore the bark canoe.

And here, by simple nature taught,
   Ere science walked abroad,
In rolling waves and thunderings,
   He heard the voice of God.

Time fled, another race appeared,
   The former passed away,
And hunters gave the lake its name,
   The name of Sabbathday.

The years rolled by, the village grew,
   The mighty forests fell.
You saw the steeple rise afar,
   You heard the Sabbath bell.

You heard the whistle of the train
   Upon its iron rails.
The wilderness was all aglow
   Along the hills and dales.

 O lovely lake, I walk thy shores,
   This calm mid-summer day,
And muse on wonders thou hast seen
   In ages passed away.

From: "The Aletheia" (1899)
by Sister Ada S. Cummings (1862–1926)
Sabbathday Lake Shaker Village, Maine.

Brothers Arnold (l) and Wayne, on an early morning walk, reflect upon the beauty and serenity of a secluded cove along the lake. They, along with their two sisters in the faith, believe the spirits of past Shakers visit them often at Chosen Land. The rippling, mirror image of the ever-changing colors of the trees upon the water is a metaphor, perhaps, for the blending of the spheres.

Sunday Meetings are open to all and are often well attended by like-minded spiritual seekers.

"Right now, we have the opportunity to preserve our land so that it remains an open space rather than be carved up into house lots and mini-malls," said Brother Wayne in 2003.

The Trust for Public Land, a national non-profit organization, took the lead and an aggressive nationwide effort to raise $3,695,000 in public and private funds was launched. The money would be used to purchase permanent conservation and preservation agreements that, according to the organization's literature, would provide funds "to cover costs and provide a mechanism to conserve the land and buildings. The two easements would allow for sustainable farming, forestry, and low-impact recreation, while prohibiting development and inappropriate uses." If the campaign proved successful, the future of Chosen Land would be secure.

Their goals were met in 2007, thanks in large part to the ever-growing 'green movement' in this country. "By putting the land in the easement," explained Brother Wayne, "it will keep its forest and agricultural use and preserve the historic buildings. It will always remain the community's property, and will alleviate the burden that future generations might have."

The burden was indeed lifted, as well as the spirits of the four Shakers who reached out to a nationwide community of like-minded preservationists and conservationists who responded to their call.

Faith

Everything old is new again

Light fills a little-used, upper-floor hall-way in the Dwelling House, built in 1883 to accommodate the Chosen Land community at its peak.

"Faith is the substance of things hoped for,
the evidence of things unseen."

HEBREWS 11:1

A Faith for Today

"Tree of Light" or "Blazing Tree" by Hannah Cohoon, 1845, Hancock Mass. Ink and watercolor on paper. 18 ⅛ x 22 9/32 inches. The inscription below the drawing reads: "The bright silver color'd blaze streaming from the edges of each green leaf, resembles so many bright torches. N.B. I saw the whole Tree as the Angel held it before me as distinctly as I ever saw a natural tree. I felt very cautious when I took hold of it lest the blaze should touch my hand. Seen and received by Hannah Cohoon in the city of Peace Sabbath Oct 9th 10th hour A.M. 1845, drawn and painted bythe same hand." Courtesy of Hancock Shaker Village, Pittsfield, Massachusetts

My journey of discovery at Chosen Land intensified on a warm October morning in 2003. The film crew hired to record the Shakers' oral histories had set up in the kitchen, and I sat across from Sister Frances at a small table by a window when the camera began to roll. As she talked, I struggled to understand why a 250-year-old faith as beautiful as Shakerism was dying out. Golden sunlight occasionally streamed through the window, the dappled light falling on a big bowl of deep red Macintosh apples recently picked from the Shakers' orchard.

The kitchen grew unusually warm, but Sister Frances kept her energy level high for two long hours that morning. She spoke with candor and passion about subjects ranging from her rebellious spirit as a teenager to the miraculous powers of the Holy Spirit. She was most enthusiastic, though, when she talked about the common ground that Shakers share with mainstream Christians. For example, she explained, Shakers believe in the Bible and study it together weekly. However, like many Christians today, the Shakers are not Fundamentalists. She wanted people to know that Shakers believe in the Ten Commandments, the power of prayer, that the Spirit can move mountains as well as peoples' souls, and that heaven is real.

I asked her to comment on the controversial belief that united America's earliest Shakers, yet also distanced them from every other Christian sect of that era. "Early Shakers believed that Mother Ann represented the Second Coming of Christ," I said. "Do you believe that?"

"No, I don't, not at all. I feel that Mother Ann had those same…" she stopped mid-sentence and picked up a tiny pamphlet she had brought with her that morning. "I want to read you something if I may," she said.

She unfolded the page and began to read. As she did, the sun that had been coming and going from behind the clouds all morning broke through with full force, showering her little pamphlet with a brilliant white light. It seemed to shimmer as Sister Frances read the following words:

"We Shakers recognize the Christ Spirit, the expression of Deity, first manifested in its fullness in Jesus of Nazareth. We also regard Ann Lee as the first to receive, in this latter day, the interior realization that the same Divine Spirit, which was in Jesus, might dwell within the consciousness of any man, woman, or child. All in whom the Christ consciousness awakens are sons and daughters of God."

She folded the page when she finished reading and looked up at me with those rays of pure, white light still streaming through the window. The entire film crew, all nine of us, witnessed the unusual light and were transfixed by its presence. I believe it was the tangible presence of the Holy Spirit, like what happened on Pentecost Sunday with the apostles. The still photographer, Jeff Toorish, a dear friend of mine, and an avowed atheist, was moved the most. He took fourteen pictures of the light on the pamphlet in Sister Frances' hands. He told me later that he took so many photographs because he, too, felt the presence of something that was "not of this world," and he wasn't sure his camera would capture it, but it did.

These days when people ask me if the Shaker faith is dying, I say, "No, not at all. The faith itself is actually undergoing a remarkable global revival, taking on a new look, in new places, in a shimmering new light."

White light showers a Shaker pamphlet read by Sister Frances during filming in 2003.

The Message

The spiritual message Ann Lee brought to America in 1774 was that everyone is capable of becoming Christ-like, and today's Shakers believe her message is just as valid today as it was more than 225 years ago. The solidity of their

A Shaker's purpose in life is to show forth Christ to all whom they may encounter. "What it will lead us to is salvation," says Brother Arnold, seen here with Brother Wayne singing during Sunday Meeting.

modern-day conviction began in the 1960s when Sister Mildred and Brother Ted joined forces to demystify, transform, and reenergize the faith. They began in 1961 by establishing *The Shaker Quarterly.* The publication (1961–1996) was a collection of essays about the life, both modern and historical and ranging from personal to scholarly, that was written primarily by Shakers. It became an important outreach for contemporary Shakers, giving them a voice in a world that many people felt had given up on them. Next came the challenging task of coming up with a 20th-century definition of the meaning and message of Shakerism. The result was Brother Ted's groundbreaking 1968 essay titled "Life in the Christ Spirit." It was not new theology, but rather solid mainstream Shakerism simply restated in a more succinct way for a modern world. In it he writes that a Shaker's purpose in life is to "show forth Christ to all whom they may encounter." He explains that God is pure Spirit, that God is love, and that love is grounded in human fulfillment by "being nothing more nor less than ourselves." He continues with, "love in the Christ spirit is beyond disillusionment for we cannot be disillusioned with people being themselves. Surely God would not have it otherwise, for it is in being ourselves—our real selves—that we are most like Christ in his sacred oneness."

"You are what you are in Shaker life. You don't wear a mask." That is how Sister Frances articulates the message of her beloved faith. For emphasis, she points to the words of an old Shaker admonition from Father James Whittaker that advises Believers to "be all that you seem to be, and seem to be what you truly are."

The Shaker message is beyond having a fixed creed because that doesn't allow room for individual interpretation. It's hard to be yourself if you subscribe to someone else's philosophy. Shakerism is organic. It needs room to grow and adjust to new situations. The message, therefore, is more aptly defined as a way of life, one that requires moment-to-moment attention. Brother Arnold puts it this way, "Shakers don't really have a theology. It isn't a study of God. Rather, it

A gentle autumn breeze lifts a vintage lace café curtain in the dining room of the Dwelling House where Sister June has set the table for the Family's evening meal.

is the practice of God. The whole reason for the life is to emulate the life of Christ. What it will lead us to is salvation."

Brother Wayne is in agreement. "One of the strengths of the Shaker faith is that everything doesn't rest on a creed." The focus is "on daily living, and the examples that Christ taught. It's not about trying to figure out all the answers in a theological sense, but living the church experience in a daily sense."

Sister Frances says the lack of a static creed is what makes it possible "for people who have already become fully involved in another church to be able to be a Shaker." Shakerism, she explains, is "just an opening for the workings of the Christ spirit, for God is working to come into our lives."

Actually living the Shaker life has always presented a radical challenge to the norm, but the challenge excludes no one. It simply asks people everywhere to unite in seeking the Father/Mother God of Love within, and to respond accordingly. It promises that doing so will help people of all creeds, even those of none, become simply more and more themselves.

Sister Frances believes Shaker life liberated her at a time when women's roles in society were quite limited. The support she received from her Shaker Family, especially during her early years, gave her the chance to become who she was meant to be. In her case, it was the opportunity to become a renowned and respected chef. In her later years she also became the leader of an internationally recognized religion, and even today in her eighties, she helps manage the Family's substantial assets and businesses.

The two major concepts of the Shaker message are unity and simplicity. Brother Ted settled on symbolism to help convey this. He chose Sister Hannah Cohoon's gift drawing "Tree of Life" to illustrate the idea of unity, and Elder Joseph Brackett's song "Simple Gifts" to illustrate simplicity. Like a tree, he wrote, the Church is organic and alive. It is "ever-changing, ever-growing, ever-adjusting to new life demands." He felt the image of a tree provided the perfect example for what he called the "vertical unity" of the Church, which Shakers believe is not rooted in time or place. Brother Ted compared the trunk of a tree to the living church here on earth, its hidden roots to the church to come, and its heavenward-stretching branches to the church triumphant that it is "united for all eternity" with God.

Unity, however, is nothing without simplicity. Elder Joseph's lyrics say that "when true simplicity is gained, to bow and to bend we shan't be asham'd," and Brother Ted agrees that humility is virtuous. He then points to the wisdom of Saint Paul, who advised us to "not think of ourselves more highly than we ought to think." Shakers believe it is only through a critical awareness of our own "simple-ness" that we come to a true understanding of our place and role in the "sacred oneness" of the body of Christ. It is upon realizing this that, in Elder Joseph's words, "we come down where we ought to be."

In this context, Sister June's comments on her relationship with God are poignant. "I experienced Him as being perfectly simple, and the way to Him is perfectly simple. You obey his commandments. I think it is a gift to see Him that simply."

". . . down where we ought to be." The Meeting House waits to fill with worshippers on a beautiful Sunday morning.

This simple, unadorned room setting (part of the museum tour) offers a glimpse a 19th century Shaker Brother's bedroom. © BRIAN VANDEN BRINK

The Shaker God

Shakers perform the religious dance "Exchange of Love" during Sunday Meeting in Mt. Lebanon, New York. Steel engraving, 1870.

Ann Lee likely held no doctrinal theological ideas about God. God was simply the essence of pure Spirit. When Spirit overwhelmed the body, a gift of God had been given. These heavenly gifts came from within, often manifesting themselves in powerful physical displays of ecstatic worship that included shaking, shouting, erratic dancing, speaking in tongues, visions, and revelations. This is what Ann Lee and her followers believed happened to them, and they actively prayed for more such gifts.

Freed by the belief in progressive revelation, the middle period of Shaker theology (1830–1890) developed the idea of God more fully. In words from a *Shaker Manifesto* written in 1880, "Our God is a living God, a God of love; but the God character manifest to mankind has widely differed, in different ages; the race has been progressing in knowledge, and with this progress there has been a change in the idea of God."

To these 19th-century Shakers, God was omniscient, omnipotent, and omnipresent, as in classic Christian theology. But the Shakers departed from traditional theology, boldly proclaiming that because God is not material and therefore has no gender, God possesses the essences of both the male and the female. Like their predecessors, they believed that in Ann Lee, God had perfectly rounded out the circle of the Christ revelation by appearing in the body of a woman.

"The way we look on God is a little different than much of the world," says Sister Frances. "We refer to God as our Father and Mother." It is a critical Shaker belief that aligns itself with ancient Gnostic concepts such as the God "within," the Father/Mother God, God is pure spirit, and God is love. This concept also appears in the emerging Postmodern Church, where followers are encouraged to push the limits on traditional notions about the nature and image of God.

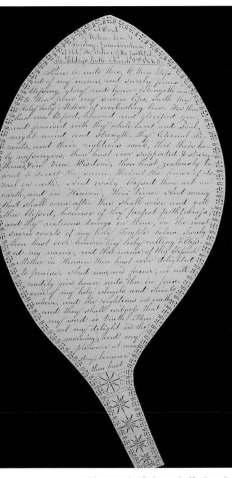

This 1845 leaf-shaped gift drawing by Sister Polly Jane Reed documents her spirit communication with "Abraham of Old."

Brother Wayne is quick to clarify the Shaker position on the duality of God. "We're not saying, 'God the Father, God the Mother.' Rather, we see God as one. We're not seeing two gods. Within all of creation there is a male and a female, so we see within God—because God is complete—that there is a masculine aspect and a feminine aspect. So we recognize that in saying our Father/Mother, but we certainly see God as one."

"God is present. God is there. God is in us. He's in you. He's in me. She is there," says Sister Frances, adding that the notion of a dual godhead always felt right to her, even as a child.

Sister June's definition of God is beautiful in its simplicity. "I believe that God is good, God is real, God is love. And the closer we are to God, the better things will be for us, and for the world."

Progressive Revelation

Progressive revelation is the constantly spinning center at the very core of the Shaker faith. Its energy allows for the reshaping of beliefs when necessary, and this has occurred several times during the history of the faith. The most recent reshaping, in the late 1960s, was initiated by Brother Ted and Sister Mildred.

Shakers believe that God continually reveals Himself/Herself as humanity is ready to receive. Sister Frances says there is no stopping place within the Shaker church. "We're expected to keep on laboring for more gifts from God, to be open to whatever changes God might have for us." The impact of this is to make each and every individual Shaker's spiritual "travel" a matter of personal salvation. "I believe I have found the path to my salvation," Brother Wayne stated with conviction in 2003.

In the earliest days, converts were discouraged from writing about their

Brothers Wayne (left) and Arnold witness morning's first light at Sabbathday Lake where they had been skipping stones. "Progressive revelation," like ripples on water, constantly moves outward in search of a new and deeper understanding of the elusive "inner light."

faith, lest they fix what should remain fluid. Preaching and other kinds of oral communication, such as hymnody, alone carried the message. When Father Joseph Meacham assumed leadership after the death of Mother Ann Lee in 1784, he took the bold step of composing and publishing *A Concise Statement* in 1790, in which he summarized the Shaker "Gospel." It was the sum and substance of the views that had brought so many converts to the emerging faith in the late 1700s.

A Concise Statement was really all about progressive revelation. It set forth the concept of four "dispensations" that God has revealed to humanity as humanity was ready to receive them. The first, the promise of Christ, was revealed to the Patriarchs; the second, the commandments, to Moses; the third, through Christ's life, death, and resurrection, to humanity, opening up

A Concise Statement (1790) is the first printed publication ever issued by the Shakers. Previously, the faith had been transmitted only by spoken word. Ann Lee and the other English founders saw print as inferior to direct oral testimonies of convinced Believers. Even those who were literate, which Ann Lee was not, felt that committing the faith to the page would dampen its dynamism.

the possibility of eternal salvation; and the fourth, the present one, the "final and last display of God's grace to a lost world" that had fallen away from the truth, was the promised second appearance of Christ. The "Second Coming" had arrived with "mighty trembling... and visions, and revelations, and prophesies." This last chance for salvation demanded of humanity "denying all ungodliness and worldly lusts; confessing all sin, and taking up the cross of Christ against the world, the flesh, and the devil."

The message that Christ had appeared this time in the body of a woman (Ann Lee) and the implications of that for the Shaker concept of God were yet to be developed publicly. The important thing was the absolute urgency of making that radical turn toward a pure and sinless life, of finding within oneself the ability to live as Christ had lived, and doing it in the here and now, "before it be too late."

With the passage of time, however, "before it be too late" lost its commanding urgency. Establishing the Kingdom of God proved to be a slower undertaking than some Shakers had thought. The idea of progressive revelation, though, only grew in meaning. It extended beyond the "dispensations" to the content of the faith itself. It empowered each Shaker to be a lone seeker, finding truth within him- or herself, and gave them the faith to evolve. It promoted a constant refinement over the years of every aspect of Shakerism. Combining with mid-19th-century ideas of evolutionary progress, it grew in sophistication. Shakerism was free to remain dynamic. It need not revere the past simply for being the past. Truth was to be sought in the present, as well.

"The beauty of Shakerism is that we believe God continually speaks to us and imparts a greater amount of wisdom to us, as we are able to understand it," says Brother Wayne. "Shakerism allows for exploration of other things, opinions, and ideas. The church doesn't see scientific advance as a threat. The view is that science merely unlocks the secrets of God's creation, rather than seeing it as a challenge to Biblical authority."

Brother Arnold, Bible in hand, enters the left side door of the Meeting House. Confession preceded attendance at Meeting in the past, but today it is much less regimented. Brother Wayne describes it as simply speaking to one of the Elders whenever the need arises, or being spoken to by one of them when the purveyor of a transgression doesn't come forth.

Belief in progressive revelation underlies 19th-century Shaker Elder Calvin Green's account of Father Joseph Meacham's vision of the "seven travels"—that the Shaker faith would move beyond even the very community Meacham had sought to build, beyond that many times over.

There are a few core beliefs, however, such as celibacy, pacifism, and communalism, one still must accept today in order to become a Shaker. A Believer can still be excommunicated, for example, for refusing to live in community or for having an affair. But fault lines are beginning to form in places where once there was only solid ground. Progressive revelation is an innately Shaker phenomenon, and with that in mind, it is never a good idea to speculate about what the faith will look like in the years to come.

Celibacy

Foremost in the modern mind as the identifying feature of Shakerism is celibacy. In early America, celibacy was the cause of severe persecution of the Shakers because it upset the traditional family structure and so had the potential to destabilized local economies. Celibacy took wives from their husbands at a time when women were considered chattal. Shakers were charged with breaking up families and this particular belief was one of the primary reasons Believers on missionary tours were whipped, stoned, or run out of an endless string of New England villages and towns. The Shaker response was always firm: Christ and the early apostles lived celibate lives, and so will we in our efforts to imitate the Christ-like life. Shakers believe celibacy frees them to enjoy the experience of a spiritual family, from which carnal relationships would have diverted them.

Justification for celibacy changed over time. Early leaders such as Father James Whitaker preached against the flesh, forcefully equating evil with the

Here, in the interior of the Dwelling House at Chosen Land, is one of many examples of how Shakers reinforced celibacy through architecture and interior design. To this day, community members reach the second-floor music room by using separate staircases, one for men and one for women. They then again enter the room through separate doors, men on the right, women on the left. Once inside, they take their seats and face each other from opposite sides of the room.

Faith

material world. In a 1785 letter to his parents back in England, he wrote, "I hate your fleshly lives, and your fleshly generation, and increasing, as I hate the smoke of the bottomless pit; and your pleading the command of God to increase and multiply, to cover your doleful corruptions; and inverting the order of heaven."

In the middle period of Shakerism (1820–1900), marriage was elevated to a necessary second-best choice: It is better to marry than to burn in hell. And there came a new element into the picture: the legal rights of women. Women's rights were so weak at this time, and Shaker belief in the equality of the sexes was so steadfast, that Shaker life promoted a flowering of selfhood in women who might otherwise have led blighted lives.

Modern Shakers do not condemn marriage. It is a common misperception that Sister Frances takes every available opportunity to shatter. "One of the greatest myths about Shakerism today is that we don't believe in marriage. We do believe in marriage. Marriage is a sacrament. God blesses marriage. God blesses sexuality. This is what makes the world go 'round. If I had not become a Shaker, I would have been married, and I certainly wouldn't feel that I was living in sin."

Today's Shakers speak loudly and clearly about the positive aspects of celibacy. In addition to freeing the individual to love all as brothers and sisters, they say it is also how God intends for us to live, as spiritual beings, in the Kingdom of Heaven. And since Shakers believe in living the Kingdom life in the here and now, celibacy is something they cherish.

Communalism

Communalism, not celibacy, is the aspect of Shaker life that people generally find the most difficult. Being part of a community requires unity, and unity requires consensus—you subordinate your own desires to the best interest of the group. Communalism also requires that you let go of all your personal possessions. "None of us owns anything but we all own everything," explains Brother Arnold.

After the death of Father James Whittaker, when Father Joseph Meacham called the first Shakers into "Gospel Order" and urged them to live and worship together, they pooled their farmland and equipment, built Meeting Houses and dwellings, and gave freely of their labor. They eventually created utopian "heavens on earth" far more bountiful than any of them could have created alone. Shaker life required industriousness, but it also offered good clothing, clean lodgings, and plenty of food.

Prayers are said before community members and staff get ready to enjoy their noon meal. Daily occasions such as this bring people together who may "have a problem" with each other, says Brother Wayne, but sitting down and talking about difficult issues "is the best way" to work through difficult situations.

Faith

As America's longest-lived and most successful experiment in communal living, this particular success story has provoked many to ask why the Shakers have been able to make communalism work when so many other groups have failed. Most answers come down to the fact that Shakers are united by their profoundly deep commitment to their faith. They depend on each other for support in their faith lives—a life far more important to them than anything else, including material possessions. "We are all here not only to attempt to work out our own salvation, but also to help each other along. Your worship, your church experience, is not a once or twice a week thing. It's a daily thing, and you have a support group with you at all times," says Brother Wayne.

Brother Arnold says the idea of communal living was always attractive to him. "I was very drawn to some kind of community, of community life." As a young man he briefly entertained the thought of joining the Sufis, but settled on the Shaker life because of what he saw at Chosen Land. "I saw a community doing its work, and the work was not just what was needed to keep the family together, it was much more important that it be embedded in their hearts. The genius of Mother Ann was to say, 'Put your hands to work, give your hearts to God. Make the two come into one.' I saw that, witnessed it, and experienced it every single visit that I made."

"I like the community life and being able to live it for God. You try not to do what you want, but what God wants you to do. Here in the community that boils down to what others want you to do. We all try to come to agreement on what we want to do," says Sister June.

For all the good things Shakers say about living in community, this aspect of Shaker life remains the biggest single reason why most novitiates leave. Brother Wayne believes it boils down to human nature. "Whether we like to admit it or not, whether we realize it or not, we're all selfish. We all like to do our own thing when we want. That can be tough, especially for

The Shakers represent America's longest-lived and most successful experiment in communal living. Here, the Family enjoys a moment of levity in the dining room.

people coming to the community who have lived alone for ten or twenty years."

Getting along with other people, putting their needs before yours, and doing it all the time is extremely difficult. When arguments or disagreements arise they need to be addressed head on, says Brother Wayne. "The really tough thing about living in community is that sometimes you think the easiest way to deal with a problem is to walk away from it and cool off. But that really doesn't resolve the issue. Sitting down and talking about it right away is the best way."

Confession

Confession has been central to Shaker life since the beginning. The first thing Ann Lee did when taking in a new convert was hear their full confession. The *Testimonies* report Ann Lee saying, "It is the heart which God looks at. The heart, with its hidden abominations, covered and concealed from the witnesses of Christ, becomes like a cage of unclean birds, and never can be cleansed short of a full and free confession." Confession, preached Fathers William and James, gave Believers the strength to move ahead and live sinless lives. Ann Lee was known for her ability to "read souls," to know whether a confession was "full and free" or whether it concealed darker truths. She was always right, said Believers who knew her.

"The confession of sin is the gateway into the church. That's the first step you have to make as a Believer," says Brother Arnold.

The *Millennial Laws* (1821) depict early Shaker life, when confession of sin, known as "opening the mind," was highly regulated. The *Laws* laid out strict rules governing the process through which Believers "purified" themselves, an act they were encouraged to perform in the presence of an Elder, as often as necessary.

In the 1940s, when Sister Frances was a child in the community, it was still called "opening the mind," but the process was much less formal. About twice a month, she recalls, Sister Mildred said to the girls, "I will be calling you tomorrow," which meant that between 9 and 10 in the morning the girls would go to her room to "open their minds." Sister Frances remembers it as a special time, when she could sit in a small Shaker chair next to Sister Mildred and pour out her heart. "She would take my hand and hold it. It was difficult sometimes to bring out feelings or things I thought I might have done wrong, but I did, and she was very understanding."

Brother Wayne describes confession in today's community as simply a matter of speaking to one of the Elders, putting right something you may have done that was wrong. "Being such a small community, someone's going to speak to you before you go to speak to someone," he says, emphasizing how the centuries-old practice has changed. "Confession brings you a sense of humiliation in a positive way because you really have to examine your conscience and your life and think about what you have done," he says. "It's good to be able to admit that you're wrong once in awhile. The big issues are always your attitude and need for adjustment because it's very easy to become self-centered, perhaps not in the traditional way, but with opinions. Some people with stronger personalities get in the habit of steamrolling over people with more meek personalities. It may not even be something you're aware of."

Sister Frances offers keen insight to modern-day people who have never experienced confession, and may have a hard time appreciating its rewards. "People today call it therapy," she says, knowing full well that most 21st-century readers will make the connection and develop a better understanding of the value and significance of this age-old tradition.

Modern Shaker confession typically takes place spontaneously, and is usually a simple matter of talking with an Elder about righting a wrong or developing ways to improve oneself. Confession, also called 'opening the mind," can occur under the shade of an elm tree or a walk to lake.

Christology

Shakers view Jesus and Mother Ann Lee as great teachers. Jesus is not "God the Son" but a beloved son of God, just as Mother Ann is a "daughter of God." They do not worship Jesus or Mother Ann, only God.

"We are Christians, but we're not Trinitarians," explains Brother Wayne. "We recognize Jesus as the great teacher who showed us the way, but we don't worship him as part of the Trinity of God. When you understand how Shakers view Jesus, you can understand how Shakers view Mother Ann. In Christ and in Mother Ann, what we have are exemplars. They are teachers. And there are others who are teachers and exemplars. To us, they have achieved the ultimate goal."

"Mother Ann herself said over and over and over, 'I am not the Christ.' I do not do these things on my own. It is the Christ spirit within me that allows me to do these things. That's what I firmly believe," states Sister Frances.

Brother Wayne says, "Mother recognized that what had been lost in the church for so long was that people began to view Jesus as doing the work of salvation for them." Mother Ann was a woman who "received the indwelling presence of the Christ spirit to the same fullness and degree that Jesus of Nazareth did." Her message, like Jesus', was meant to awaken humanity to the work that humanity itself—not Jesus or Mother—was supposed to do. "We don't have people doing the work of salvation for us," stresses Brother Wayne, adding that Jesus and Mother Ann were simply two great teachers, among many others, who showed humanity first-hand how to actually do the work of saving one's soul.

The Shaker perspective on the Second Coming of Christ is also different from many other Christian faiths, and is considered vastly misunderstood. Shakers believe the Second Coming is a personal experience that happens when an individual quietly accepts the anointing spirit of God, which, in Brother Ted's words in *Life in the Christ Spirit* is "the spirit of love and truth."

Mother Ann is recorded as saying "The second appearing of Christ is in His Church." Sister Frances agrees that the return of the Spirit happens within individuals who collectively make up the 'church.' She says, "It's a very quiet coming of the Christ within individuals who are open to it. It can happen more than once."

"When we make Jesus Christ and his ministry manifested in our lives through our daily living," Brother Wayne says, "that is how Christ reappears constantly. As Paul tells us in his Epistles, we "are the body of Christ." The body is the church. The body is made up of Believers, and all of us have our own gifts that we bring just like in any body. There are eyes, ears, toes, and hearts. We all bring our different gifts. And just as an individual organ can't

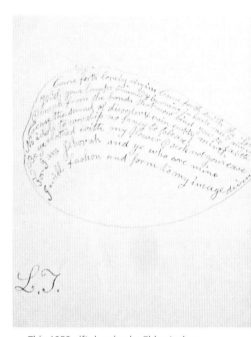

This 1850 gift drawing by Elder Joshua Bussell shows an angel trumpeting the verse, "Come forth lovely virgins, Come forth saith the Lord . . ."

survive without the rest of the body, neither can the body survive without that organ. It shows us how we're all dependent upon each other to make the body work."

The Bible

The Bible plays an important role in Shaker life. A copy rests on the nightstand of every Believer. Morning and noontime prayers include the reading of select passages. Shakers participate in weekly Bible study classes, and every Sunday Meeting begins and ends with readings from the Old and New Testaments. They view the Bible as a historical document and a work of great spiritual importance. "Everything we do is formed in the Gospels. It is that New Testament theology that we're striving to live," says Brother Arnold.

Nonetheless, Shakers are not biblical literalists, and they believe it is limited by the understanding of those who wrote it. The book, says Brother Wayne, is better read as "a constant progression of man's understanding of God's will for him" than to be consulted on matters scientific. He goes on to say, "We use the Bible as a guide for our life of faith because within it are the teachings essential for a Christian life. Overall we view it as the word of God as man understood it at that time and place. Again, that's where you see the evolution of progressive revelation."

Sister June feels guided by the Spirit.

Spiritualism

Shakers seek to live close to the spirit world, and they welcome occasions when the veil between the two worlds is lifted.

"I think Sister Mildred (1897–1990) is still here in the spirit a lot," says Sister June. "You can feel her presence, especially in Sunday Meeting. It just seems like there are a lot more people there than you can actually see. I have a feeling these people, who were here for so many years and contributed so much, probably come to visit quite often. They care about us, they are probably praying for us, and watching over us."

Sister June says she can even feel the presence of the Holy Spirit inside her in a physical way. "It keeps me warm, even if it's a cold day," she claims. "And I have a sense of protection, as though I have a shield around me, and nothing hurts me. I have a sense that someone is there within me, and since I've been here I've had the feeling it's been growing, and that I am guided by the Spirit. I'm grateful for it."

"I have always believed that I have a guardian angel," says Sister Frances, who often testifies in Sunday Meeting about how the angel helps and guards her.

The stories these two Shakers tell is not unlike those told by Believers who lived during what's known as the Era of Manifestations (1837–1850). It was a time of intense religious and spiritual activity in all Shaker communities that predated, by almost a full generation, the larger American Spiritualist movement.

During the Era of Manifestations, also known as the Era of Mother's Work, entire Shaker communities, including children, sought to encounter, some through trance, those who had passed over to the spirit world. Shakers who were especially sensitive were able to "interpret" the Spirit's message. They were known as mediums or "instruments." This "gift" of interpretation was the source of a tremendous outpouring of mystical art and music, most of which is now highly regarded as prized examples of American folk art.

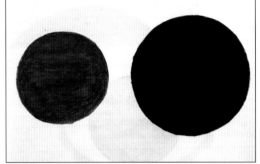

Detail of Miranda Barber's 1843 gift drawing depicting of one of the signs of the "end times" foretold in the Bible's Book of Revelation. She wrote these words to accompanying the image, "The Sun clothed in Sackcloth and the Moon in Scarlet!!! Heavy Judgements shall come on the Earth I will avenge mine Anger upon Men!! Saith the Lord of Hosts."

From "A Book of prophetic signs written by Prophet Isaiah, 1843," by Miranda Barber, Mt. Lebanon, NY. Ink, watercolor and graphite on paper, leather-bound. Pages size: 8 1/2 x 6 13/16 in. Courtesy of The Western Reserve Historical Society, Cleveland, Ohio.

The cemetery at Chosen Land has but one communal headstone. Shakers believe a person's material body decays upon death, but their spirit is eternal and continues on—in this world and the beyond.

The Afterlife

Shakers believe that at death the material body decays, but the spirit is eternal and moves on. "We believe there is a hereafter," says Brother Arnold. Shaker funerals, not surprisingly, are primarily a celebration of the individual's life. All members of the community participate fully, as do friends and family from near and far. After the ceremony, says Sister Frances, "the family follows the hearse down to the cemetery. Everyone stands for final prayers, and then, for the Shakers and anyone else who is inclined, a little dirt is picked up and put into the hole before it's covered up."

While "from dust to dust" may be the body's fate, such is not the spirit's. Shakers believe some spirits, such as that of Mother Ann, gain immediate entrance into heaven upon their death. This is the kind of glorious salvation Shakers believe can be achieved by a full-fledged living of the Kingdom Life. "We're starting the work now so that we don't have to do it later in the afterlife," explains Brother Arnold.

Shakers believe the work of salvation will continue in the afterlife for spirits that are not yet ready for heaven, and that these spirits can benefit from the prayers of the living to speed up the process. Mother Ann spoke empathetically of the pain of the departed who had not entered heaven, and she prayed intensely, or "bore for" them, to help them on their way.

Brother Wayne concurs. "I think your struggle to be one with God is something that goes on forever, not only in this life, but certainly in the afterlife."

Shakers do not believe their faith life is a higher calling than any other Christian religion, but they do believe living the Kingdom Life will grant them, or anyone, quicker entrance into heaven. They also do not believe they are God's "chosen" people. In fact, it is quite the opposite; Shakers believe it is they who choose to follow God.

Likewise, Shakers do not believe salvation is an exclusive club open to members of one particular church or religion. "God judges you on the merit of your life," Brother Wayne says. "I think if you're a person of good conscience, whether you embrace the Christian faith or another faith, God meets you and deals with you where you are. It seems to me that when we talk about a merciful God, and how God loves us. . . and then you think, well, five billion other people in the world are damned because they don't follow my particular sect. . . it doesn't make sense. It's presumptuous to say you know the mind of God; that you can walk around and say, 'I'm the elect of God,' because ultimately it's God's decision; God takes into account your life. It's not just about your creeds and forms, but rather it's the daily life and the changes that you make in life."

Misty cove on Sabbathday Lake. Shakers are not biblical literalists. They are encouraged to continually reevaluate their understanding of Holy Scripture. Brother Wayne gives this example of how progressive revelation works, as it relates to an individual's interpretation of the Bible: "The Bible speaks of the four corners of the world, and when Christ walked the earth everyone believed the world was flat. Well," he says of later knowledge to the contrary, "a circle doesn't have corners." Hence the need for a life-long pursuit of a deeper understanding of God's will for mankind.

Faith

Worship
'...as the Spirit may lead you'

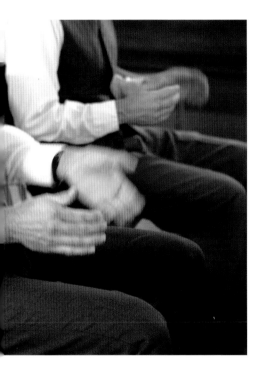

The Shaker Brothers' hands clapping in unison to "Followers of the Lamb," a favorite hymn among Shakers and non-Shaker's alike. Photo taken inside the 1794 Meeting House at Chosen Land.

"Let them praise His name in the dance: let them sing praises unto him...."

PSALM 149:3

The Gifts of the Spirit

Morning sun illuminates the inner shelf of the podium inside the Winter Chapel in the Dwelling House. The Shakers' Alter Services book, juxtaposed by a rising thermometer, is the same one used during many other Christian services, as well.

Worship at Chosen Land is mysterious and unpredictable, like wind blowing through the branches of the maple trees that grow throughout the village. You never know what to expect. The Spirit, having a likewise will of its own, makes its presence known mysteriously and unpredictably through Believers themselves, using their bodies as sacred vessels and their voices to deliver messages from the world beyond. It is considered a gift from above when it occurs, but it can only happen after the individual has totally and completely surrendered to the higher power.

In the unstructured early years of Shakerism, the presence of the Spirit manifested itself as frenzied, erratic body movements that usually occurred while a Believer was in a trance-like state of worship. Mother Ann and her followers often flailed their limbs unpredictably while their heads jerked back and forth and side to side. They sang haunting, mysterious "wordless songs" such as "lo-de-lo" and "ve-um vum vum," and they spoke in unknown tongues. It lasted last for hours, sometimes even days. The Shakers' twisting and turning round and round until they dropped to the floor in complete exhaustion was the source of considerable scorn and ridicule, but it never shook their faith in the power of the Holy Spirit. In fact, it was precisely what they were looking for. It was evidence to them that heaven and earth grew closer.

Shakerism was America's earliest experience with the outward display of the "gifts of the Spirit," as described by St. Paul in his letter to the Corinthians (12:8-11.) Its most recent is Pentecostalism, with more than 250 million adherents around the world. The modern-day worship of Pentecostals, like that of the first Shakers, can often include speaking in tongues, ecstatic praise, prophecy, faith healing, and belief in miracles. The Pentecostal movement, which includes several Christian denominations, gained additional "legitimacy" in the 1960s and early 70s with the emergence of the Charismatic movement. Both Pentacostals and Charismatics, like Shakers, believe the manifestations of the Holy Spirit, the so-called "gifts of the Spirit," are available to anyone who is willing to follow its lead. When combining the number of Charismatics with Pentecostals, membership totals nearly a quarter of the world's two billion Christians. They share many, although not all, beliefs with America's Shakers.

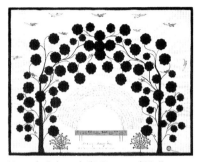

Hannah Cohoon's "A Bower of Mulberry Trees, 1854." Among Shakers, the bower was symbol of willing submission to divine purposes. Courtesy of Hancock Shaker Village, Pittsfield, Massachusetts.

During the Era of Manifestations the Spirit made itself known among Shakers in different ways. The gifts of the Spirit were deliberate and purposeful, oftentimes coming directly from Mother Ann herself (now in the Spirit world) offering guidance and direction to new generations of Shakers. This era of intense religious activity in all Shaker villages is also referred to as the period of "Mother Ann's Work." It was a rich atmosphere that produced a prolific gush of music, dance, and drawings, and reenergized many Shaker communities at a time when membership was waning. "Simple Gifts" is one such song among a remarkable ten thousand Shaker songs believed to hail from heavenly spheres. The creative outpouring also produced an estimated two hundred gift drawings. The Shakers kept these drawings secret for many years because of their mystical nature, fearing they would be misunderstood and prompt public ridicule. Ironically, these once private and highly guarded works of divinely inspired creativity later become the source of many iconic images of America itself. One drawing in particular, "The Tree of Life" by Hannah Cohoon in 1854, was featured on a 1974 UNICEF Christmas postcard.

The nature of a spiritual gift, according to Shaker lore, allows for it to be withdrawn when its purpose has been served. The widespread 'shaking' gift of the early days seems to have been replaced by artistic gifts in the 19th century. It's much more difficult to define what spiritual gifts were bestowed upon Shakers in the 20th century, although some say it was "quietude and contemplation."

The Story Behind the Shakers' Most Famous Song: 'Simple Gifts'

Joseph Brackett, Jr. (1797–1882) received the "gift" of this song in 1848 "during a time of great tribulation for him," explains Brother Arnold. As an Elder in the Maine Ministry, he and his assistant, Elder Otis Sawyer, were required to spend their time equally at the state's two Communities (Alfred and Sabbathday Lake) and when he learned that Elder Otis was being transferred out of state he was heartbroken. A Shaker journal entry indicates his sadness was over having to "tread the wine press alone" because there were no Brethren left in the state who were able to help him lead.

Much folklore surrounds the song that is now world famous, but none of the conflicting tales have ever been supported. One story written in a manuscript at Lebanon says the tune was given to Elder Brackett from a "Negro" spirit at Canterbury. Another is from an Eldress at Hancock who says she remembers seeing Elder Brackett sing "Simple Gifts" in a meeting room there, turning about "with his coat tails a-flying."

**'Tis the gift to be simple,
'Tis the gift to be free;
'Tis the gift to come down
where we ought to be;
And when we find ourselves
in the place just right,**

'Twill be in the valley
of love and delight.
When true simplicity is gained,
To bow and to bend
we shan't be ashamed.
To turn, turn will be our delight,
'Til by turning, turning
we come around right.

Sister Mildred with Composer Aaron Copeland in Shaker Heights, Ohio in 1974. Sr. Mildred, Sr. Frances, and Br. Ted were in Ohio to conduct seminars during the Shaker bicentennial. They were invited to attend a birthday party for Mr. Copeland. He gave Sr. Mildred an autographed copy of his arrangement of "Simple Gifts."

Elder Joseph Brackett, Jr. served alone in the Maine Ministry until 1859 when he was appointed the First Elder at Chosen Land, a position he served with honor until 1880. He passed away two years later at the age of 83.

He never knew his little song, received through divine inspiration during the darkest days of his life, would come to permeate American culture; with adaptations and variations ranging from TV theme songs to football fight songs, from Broadway to the symphony. The most recent, and widest-reaching performance ever of a rendition of "Simple Gifts" came during the January 20, 2009 Inauguration of President Barack Obama. Titled "Air and Simple Gifts," it was composed by the legendary John Williams and included world-famous performers Yo-Yo Ma and Itzhak Perlman.

Equally impressive was an adaptation of "Simple Gifts" that made its way into Aaron Copeland's ballet suite "Appalachian Spring." He received the 1945 Pulitzer Prize for Music for this suite that included a Shaker-inspired rendition.

Gifts aside, the 20th century marked what historians say was the beginning of the end for Shakerism. Membership declined rapidly, and the number of villages shrank from 19 in 1827 to 6 in 1925. Today, there is only one active village—Chosen Land.

It is my belief, however, that the numbers do not tell the whole story. I believe the viability of the Shaker faith lies in the number of Christians who practice the beliefs, or at least a majority of the beliefs. There are a lot of Catholics, for example, who are "counted" as members of the church, even though they do not practice all the beliefs—such as abortion, or they support gay marriage. When viewed in this light, the Shaker faith deserves a second look with respect to its rightful place on America's religious landscape. The time has come to take Shakerism off the endangered species list and acknowledge its common ground with millions, even billions of Christians worldwide.

There's no question among historians that the Shakers left a permanent mark on America's cultural landscape. One of the ways they did it, or "do" it in the case of the living Shakers at Chosen Land, is by holding fast to their unique style of worship. No other distinctly American religion can lay claim to such a widely varied and internationally acclaimed body of creative works as Shakerism can, and today interest has never been greater. Despite all this, the faith that animated the movement has never been well understood.

I believe that's changing, though. As we push forward in the 21st century, awareness of religion and spirituality is increasing. There's a bona fide hunger these days for a deeper understanding of the meaning of life, and millions of people have discovered that broadening their theological perspective is as easy as going online. Chosen Land went online (www.shaker.lib.me.us) in the early 1990s, and their site continues to be a critical tool for communicating the message and meaning of modern Shakerism. Additionally, Web sites devoted to religion, faith, and spirituality are among the most visited, drawing the attention of people of all faiths, or no faith. These "virtual" church communities are connecting millions of people who report they prefer exploring spirituality online because its anonymous nature provides a safe haven for the theologically curious. One simply cannot be shamed, shunned, or excommunicated from a virtual church for asking tough questions or seeking out non-conforming religious information.

I believe the Holy Spirit is saving the best "gift" till last. It will be less tangible than gifts of the past, but it will be more powerful and more awe-inspiring than all the other gifts combined. I believe it's coming, not on clouds of righteousness, but through technology that will increasingly connect millions of people worldwide who are open to the leading of the Spirit and its bounty of gifts.

I'm grateful to Brother Ted and Sister Mildred for their efforts in the 1960s to reopen Sunday Meeting at Chosen Land to the public. I'm grateful they held fast to traditional Shaker worship when it was dropped altogether in the 1930s at the only other active Shaker village in the country in Canterbury, New Hampshire (1792–1992). I'm grateful that I long ago surrendered to the Spirit that called me to Chosen Land even though I have been ridiculed for worshiping there and criticized for taking my children with me. Nothing can shake my faith in the power of the Holy Spirit, and I have the Shakers at Chosen Land to thank for this not-so-simple gift.

Worship gathers together another community: the non-Shakers whose presence is actively honored, and who clearly gain something from the experience or would not return again and again. Sara Langseth (front center) of Warwick, Rhode Island, worships with the Shakers several times a year. She is seated next to her mother, Jo-Ann Langseth, also of Warwick. Sara's father, Rich Langseth, is with them, but he is sitting with the Brothers on the other side of the Meeting House. Here, parishioners prepare to sing a "set song" from a Shaker hymnal.

The Parishioners

A small group of about a dozen people, mostly locals from neighboring towns, regularly attends Sunday Meeting with the Shakers at Chosen Land. A few of them make a three-hour drive from their homes in Massachusetts to be with the Shakers in Maine at least once a month. Two or three have been

"We encourage people to worship with us because if they really want to understand the Shakers, that is where it should begin." —Brother Wayne

worshiping with the Shakers for more than twenty years and have developed deep, long-lasting friendships with them.

"We've come to call them our parishioners because we don't know what else to call them," says Brother Wayne with a grin. "They very actively participate during worship. They testify. They learn all the songs and can sing along with us. It makes a nice addition."

The parishioners are a fascinating collection of free-thinking spiritual seekers made up of school teachers, retirees, a graphic artist, a professor, homemakers, mothers and fathers, college students, business owners, blue-collar workers, and an occasional teenager sporting body piercing. Most are married, a few are single, one or two are gay. Someone new drops in from time to time. Some wear suits, others wear dress slacks or skirts, most wear denim, all are welcome.

"It is a real blessing that all these people have begun coming to Meeting," says Sister Frances. "I find it very helpful when I hear people speak during Meeting. I'm very moved, and I want to take to heart what they have said."

She has a hunch about what is drawing increasing numbers of people, especially young people, to Meeting. "So many [of them] have become disillusioned with going to church because they just sit there and they are preached 'to.' Young people tell me this. At our Meetings, everyone is free to participate."

The increase in attendance among "Postmodern-type" Christians may also have a lot to do with Shaker tolerance and ecumenicalism. "Everybody is welcome, no matter what," stresses Sister Frances. "Shakers are taught to regard every person without discrimination because it might be the Christ. We have people coming to us from every walk of life. We have one person who is Catholic, and she goes to Mass on Saturday so she can be here on Sunday for Meeting. We [also] have a friend who is an Orthodox Jew who comes every single year. He leaves New York City at three o'clock in the morning in order to be here in time for service. It's amazing."

During the summer tourist season the population in Maine can swell by nearly half a million people, many of whom live in their "camps" and summer homes several months at a time. Figures are hard to come by, but an estimated 100 people actually refer to the Shaker church as their church during the summer. "They come every single Sunday that they are in Maine," says Sister Frances with pride. "Route Twenty-Six is lined with cars."

Brother Wayne is pragmatic about why some people come to Sunday Meeting. "I think a lot of people come out of curiosity. Some of it is good curiosity, some of it is bad curiosity," he says. "Once in a while we'll get an Evangelical who'll want to 'save us' and everyone else in the congregation. That [happens] about once every two years. That's nice. At least they care," he says tongue in cheek. He notes that Shaker church is like other churches in that parishioners come and go. "We've had people who might be with us for five or six years, then they either move away or start attending another church."

Regardless why "world's people" attend or stop attending Sunday Meeting, there is a sense among the Shakers that most people get something from

Ken Averill of Massachusetts shares fellowship and a smile with Brother Arnold following Sunday Meeting. Ken and his wife Mary have been coming to Chosen Land for more than fifteen years.

simply being there. "I think it's wonderful that our worship services are open to the public," says Sister Frances, who remembers the days prior to 1961 when this was not so. "They may not want to be a Shaker, but they found something in that Meeting room that helps them go on with their lives. It could have been exactly what they have been looking for."

Sunday Best

The Shakers at Chosen Land wear traditional Shaker clothing at Sunday Meeting. "We tend to dress a little more traditionally for worship," says Brother Wayne. "It's basically putting on your Sunday clothes, but ours tend to be just a little more traditional. I wear a white shirt and a vest unless it's cold, then I wear a suit jacket and dress slacks."

"When the Shakers first came from England and settled in New York," explains Sister Frances, "the traditional dress that women wore was a long dress down to their ankles. Some of them wore shawls around it. Because one of the tenets of the Shaker faith is simplicity, it was decided that they would accept whatever dress was worn then, and not change with the styles."

Shaker fashion, nonetheless, did change over time. Mildred Barker was the last Sister to wear a Shaker cap, for example. Additionally, hems rose on Sisters' dresses, colors changed, and fabrics were updated to include permanent press. The dresses worn at Chosen Land today were made by hand by a friend of the community who passed away four years ago. The Sisters gave her input on color and fabric selection, but the style has remained consistent for at least two generations.

What is most notable about today's Shaker dress is the full cape that covers the bodice front and back. Sister Frances explains its purpose. "When you begin to gain some shape, that is when the girls were put into Shaker dresses.

Sisters Frances and June worship in traditional Shaker clothing. "I love the Shaker dress," says Sister Frances.

The females were pretty much covered up, up here. I guess it was part of the celibacy, not to be attractive to the opposite sex."

Like most people, the Shakers are quick to change out of their Sunday best as soon as Meeting is over. Their non-Shaker clothes are like everyone else's.

Sunday Meeting

There is a prescribed order to the unfolding of a Shaker Sunday Meeting that lies in sharp contrast to the spontaneous, charismatic "leading of the Spirit" so strongly encouraged during worship itself.

Sister June is the first Shaker to walk from the Dwelling House, cross Route 26, and go up the granite steps to the Meeting House. She enters through the narrow double doors on the right side of the unassuming "house church." Her arrival is about fifteen minutes before the service actually begins, and there are usually several other people already there. Sister June takes her seat on a long honey-colored bench that marks the first of several rows of identical benches. Shaker hymnals rest on the benches like place cards awaiting the arrival of worshipers. It is quiet.

Sister Frances and Brother Arnold, the Elders and spiritual leaders of the community, arrive together shortly after, each having entered through a gender-specific door. The Meeting House fills quickly with non-Shakers during the summer due to the tremendous influx of tourists into the area. Attendance from June through August may exceed one hundred people.

Brother Wayne is the last to arrive. "I ring the bell outside at ten a.m.," he says, explaining that he tolls the massive cast iron bell seven times "because seven is a very spiritual number."

Brother Arnold always offers a greeting when it's obvious there are newcomers in attendance. "We'd like to welcome you all to Sunday Meeting," he

Brother Wayne tolls the bell alerting all that Sunday Meeting is about to begin.

Sunlight streaming through the windows
of the Meeting House creates a warm
and welcoming presence.
© Brian Vanden Brink.

says in a pleasant tone, "and we encourage you to participate in song or testimony as the Spirit may lead you. Mother Ann said a strange gift never came from God, so please don't feel strange or be a stranger."

Each Shaker then stands in turn at the podium to read a Bible passage. Sister June begins the Meeting with a "call to worship"—the reading of a Psalm from the Bible. Sister Frances then announces the first "set song" from the hymnal, which is chosen ahead of time to harmonize with the readings, and everyone is invited to join the Shakers in song. Next, Brother Arnold reads a passage from the Old Testament. Brother Wayne reads from the New Testament, "usually an epistle from either Paul, Peter, James, or John," he notes. Sister Frances is the last to read from the podium; a Gospel selection. The readings are selected according to standard guidelines used by most Protestant churches. "After that we have another 'set song,' Sister Frances says.

"From there we go forth and explore the lessons in the readings," Brother Wayne says, setting the stage for "laboring," which is unequivocally the single most important outward aspect of Sunday Meeting.

A puff of wind gathers under the "modesty bib" of Sister June's traditional Shaker dress as a friend escorts her up the granite steps of the Meeting House; an omen, perhaps, suggesting an uplifting Sunday service.

Laboring for "Inner Light"

"One of the things I noticed right away in coming to Shaker Meeting back when I was young," said Brother Wayne, "was the fact that at other churches, the priest or minister stands up and tells you 'these are the readings and this is what we're going to learn from them.'"

Shaker testimony during Sunday Meeting is the active pursuit of the elusive "inner light," a metaphor for the knowledge of God.

He prefers Shaker Sunday worship because "you hear the readings and then you try to figure out what's going on." Brother Wayne is referring to the time during meeting when people stand up and speak publicly, or "testify," sharing their thoughts and insights on the Scripture just read.

"When you really have to think about what the readings are trying to say," he continues, "I think you develop a greater sense because you're actively participating. You're actively seeking out the message of God. Laboring is seeking out God."

Sister Frances says giving testimony isn't always easy, but that's not the point. "My role is to begin the testimonies. I speak first," she explained, referring to her role as the Eldress, the female leader of the community. But, she said, "there are times when I would like not to. There are times when I like to sit there to hear the readings, to be a part of the music, but I don't feel especially bound to give testimony. But that wouldn't be right, particularly since we're so few, and since I am in the position that I am. That is what is expected of me, so that is what I do. I labor. I labor to have God put the words into my heart that I will be saying with my tongue when I testify. That's one form of laboring, to not just sit there and leave it all up to others. You have to labor to do what is expected of you."

Laboring should not be limited to Sunday Meeting, says Brother Wayne. "You should constantly be trying to understand God's will."

The act of testifying, the very public nature of it, combined with a vigorous internal struggle to labor for spiritual truths often triggers the release of a flood of emotions. It's not uncommon for worshipers to weep during testimony, both as the one speaking and as listeners. This is true for Shakers as well as non-Shakers. Sunday Meeting is a safe place for people of all faiths to explore not only the word of God, but the meaning of their individual lives as well.

There is an unwritten code among those who worship regularly with the Shakers: what happens in Meeting stays in Meeting. Testimony is sacred. It is blessed by the Spirit. It is personal and intimate. And for that reason, the Shakers do not allow photography, still or video, during testimony.

Shakers and world's people prepare to "labor" during Sunday Meeting in a setting and according to traditions that have remained virtually unchanged since 1794.

Singing

Sunday Meeting is a rare gem with many sparkling facets, not the least of which is the spontaneous "offering up" of Shaker song following someone's testimony. "It's almost like saying 'Amen,'" says Sister Frances, to what someone has just said.

She gives this example to demonstrate how the gift works: "If someone mentions a special goal they want to attain spiritually, it strikes a chord. If I begin a song, it is not in my head ahead of time." She claims the motivation and inspiration for the choice of song comes directly and unequivocally from the Spirit. It is the essence of the meaning of following "the leading of the Spirit." And not a Meeting goes by without tapping into a treasure trove of Shaker hymnody, received from the spirit world, for the exclusive benefit of Believers. It is a powerful spiritual tool.

"These songs have all come from Believers who have lived this life and made it a point to seek that Kingdom of God on earth. When I am in Meeting I feel the spirits of all those people who have gone before. It is a gift from God," says Sister Frances.

She's not alone in that belief. Sister June claims to feel the presence of Sister Mildred in many Meetings. The mystical, rhythmic, rhapsodic quality of many of the songs no doubt contributes to her feeling.

Another facet to the gem of Shaker song, one that still exists today, is movement. A few Shaker "motion songs" (hymns accompanied by predetermined clapping, simple hand gestures, and occasional foot stomping) are frequently offered up following testimony. Although the movement is dramatically limited compared to the frenzy of ecstatic worship, there appears to be no limit to the spiritual joy felt by Believers when singing popular songs.

There are an estimated 10,000 Shaker hymns. Even more remarkable than the sheer volume of tunes is the fact that the vast majority of these songs

Two pre-selected "set songs" are sung from Shaker hymnals during the first part of the Meeting. They precede spontaneous singing that can be "offered up" by anyone during testimony. All singing is a cappella.

were passed down orally, like precious family heirlooms from one generation of Shakers to the next.

Gift Drawings

Looking at gift drawings provides another angle from which to view the Shaker faith. Believers produced these mysterious works during the middle of the 19th century while under the influence of spiritual trances. They assigned credit to the Spirit, not the individual. The images are said to be glimpses of the sights and sounds of the world beyond—both heaven and hell—and today's Shakers accept them as such.

"It must have been something the Spirit gave them to help them in their spiritual life," is how Sister June sees it.

Credit for bringing these artistic interpretations of the spirit world, literally and figuratively, "out of the closet" of the Shakers belongs to antique dealers Edward Demming Andrews and his wife, Faith. They were traveling the back roads of New England in 1923 searching for treasures when they discovered the Shakers at Hancock Village, in Massachusetts. What they saw, "a trestle table, benches, rocking chairs, built-in cupboards, cooking arches, all beautiful in their simplicity," wrote Edward later, whetted their appetites for more. The couple befriended the Shakers, and began buying up all the old hand-made furniture they could find, which was often stacked to the rafters in the Shakers' barns, basements, and attics. Both parties were happy, especially the Andrews, who believed they could invent a market for what they found.

In 1927, Edward was asked to write an article in *Antiques* magazine extolling the virtues of the Shaker esthetic in furniture design, and from that moment forward, he and his wife reportedly became obsessed with collecting and reselling everything Shaker. Edward's "buying" relationship with the

Gift drawing and gift poem from the collection at Chosen Land. The creators of these divinely inspired works of art are unknown. Both are circa 1850, and from the Shaker Village in Mt. Lebanon, New York.

Shakers continued for years, and his eventual discovery of their once-private gift drawings solidified his and Faith's position as the original premier purveyors of Shaker material culture. They are credited with renewing America's interest in Shakerism by promoting and selling Shaker material culture. The couple is often sharply criticized for capitalizing on the situation by not being honest with the Shakers about how much they thought they could get at market for their goods. On the other hand, if a less savvy antiques dealer, or no one at all, had stumbled upon the Shakers back in the 1920s perhaps they would have disappeared without notice.

Less than two hundred gift drawings are known to exist. Most are displayed in museums or are in private collections. Six are in the collection at the Sabbathday Lake Shaker Library at Chosen Land, including "A Gift From Mother Ann to Eldress Eunice" received by Polly Collins of Hancock Shaker Village in Massachusetts in 1859.

Mother Ann is recorded as saying, "Speak but little about your spiritual gifts, . . . those beautiful gifts I have given you for your comfort and encouragement in the way of God." One can only hope she is pleased that nearly two hundred gift drawings, "seen and received" by her followers, entered America's cultural mainstream, and in the process became sources of divine inspiration to new generations of people in search of a deeper understanding of the power and influence of the Spirit.

Ecstatic Worship

Many changes have occurred over the course of Shakerism regarding ecstatic worship—the free and unencumbered physical expression of the manifestation of the Spirit. From its wild, erratic, sometimes chaotic beginnings among the earliest Shakers, to the ritualized and highly rehearsed spiritual dances of the early 1800s, to the simple hand movements and foot stomping accompanying today's motion songs, what is most important is simply the fact that it remains.

Brother Arnold explains the changes that have occurred regarding ecstatic worship and dance:

"In the time of Mother and the Elders (1774–1784) there was no such thing as we think of as the 'dance.' It was all ecstatic worship. It was whirling, twirling, it was running, it was leaping, it was dancing, it was rolling on the floor. Nothing discernible as a 'dance' was part of their worship."

That (Shaker "dance") came about with an increase in order that comes with the establishment of the church into Gospel homes (in the 1790s.) And then, indeed, there were dances. The early dances tended to be very lively, spirited, and quick. These eventually evolved into something a little less lively. Then they developed into marches, which were more graceful and stately, but

These photographs were taken in 1905 as part of a series of images demonstrating 19th-century dance movements used during Shaker worship. The woman featured was not a Shaker, but rather the author of an article that appeared in *Connecticut Magazine* (Vol. 9, No 4), entitled "Spirituality as Expressed in Song." Courtesy of Fruitlands Museum, Inc. Harvard Massachusetts.

Several rows of Shakers, separated by gender, performing a step dance in the meeting hall at New Lebanon, New York. Lithograph, circa 1830.

definitely slower. Finally, they devolved into something so slow, they were called a "walking march." So, by the 1890s the communities had more or less felt that the gift was up, (withdrawn) as it were, for dances.

The reason for a lack of movement in worship was the dynamic it took. It took a lot of coordination. It took a lot of commitment and a lot of vigor, and many of the communities didn't have it. The turnover was too great. The older members were indeed old, and these people wouldn't have been marching in Meetings anyhow. They would have been sitting it out."

A recently released twenty-minute DVD titled "We Find No Harm In Dancing" offers an excellent and historically accurate glimpse into the world of Shaker dance. In the film, the highly respected performing arts group The Enfield Shaker Singers demonstrates the beauty of Shaker dance as it was performed nearly two hundred years ago. The group is under the direction of Shaker song and dance expert Mary Ann Haagen and it has performed throughout New England to the delight of thousands.

The Last Ecstatic Dance

No one has "shaken" under the influence of the Holy Spirit during Shaker Meeting in a very long time. The word "shake" itself is an insufficient description for what can happen when a Believer surrenders his or her will to that of the Spirit, opening a portal into their soul.

Sister Frances is the only person alive to have witnessed the gift of a Shaker being swept up by ecstatic worship. It is a sacred story, one she tells with power and conviction. The year was 1938.

Although spontaneous movement during worship in the 21st century is limited to Shaker "motion songs" (hymns accompanied by clapping, simple hand gestures, and occasional foot stomping), there is no limit to the spiritual joy felt by Believers when offering up these popular songs.

"I remember a very, very moving experience. I had not yet moved into the Dwelling House so I was probably between the ages of ten and eleven. It happened upstairs in the Winter Chapel [in the Dwelling House].

"Picture this, if you will. In the front of the chapel was Eldress Prudence, Sister Jenny, Eldress Harriet, and Brother Delmer. They faced the congregation because they were the Elders, they were the hierarchy within the church. And then there were probably six or seven benches with people on each bench. The older sisters, the ones who really had come through, were on the front benches and then they gradually went up until there was a bench for little girls, and then a little row of chairs for the very tiny children five or six years old.

"It was very full, and Meeting was going along, and it must've been a very good Meeting because all of a sudden that Spirit penetrated the Meeting. I want you to remember there were all these young people. There were a few boys also at that time. All of a sudden it was quiet, and Sister Eliza Jeffers was brought abruptly to her feet. She was the most unassuming, gentle person I've ever known—she was 70. She had very blue eyes and white hair piled up in a little bun on her head. All of a sudden she began to whirl. She began to go around in a circle.

"Eldress Prudence immediately left her seat, went over to Sister Eliza, never touched her, but just circled her so that. . . I mean, if this was God-given, God was going to keep her protected, but perhaps Eldress Prudence didn't real-ize that. . . didn't want her falling on a bench, or something. Eldress Prudence just circled her and stayed right there. Sister Eliza was in front and there were benches between us, but she was just sort of whirling around and around and around. She was on her feet. I believe her eyes were closed. It only lasted a few minutes.

"And then I remember seeing Sister Eliza. She was pale as a ghost. She sat down. Remember what I told you about the Meeting room being filled? There was not a sound; not one snicker or gasp from a young person; not from the

Sister Eliza Jeffers, seen here sitting on a porch at Chosen Land with her visiting nephew and niece, was the last Shaker to experience spontaneous ecstatic "movement of the Spirit" during worship.

boys; complete silence. It was toward the end of meeting, and after a brief interval, someone else got up and spoke and meeting continued. And when it was over, we just filed out. Everyone filed out in absolute silence. I'll never forget, the children just left and went back to their house in complete silence. It was overwhelming. It really was. I was very moved.

"I wasn't frightened, but I was certainly caught up in it. Everyone must've been. Because, you'd expect children, or even the little girls to say 'Ohhhhh!' or something, but there was nothing. Nothing. Absolute silence. That was the last manifestation of the Spirit that has ever happened in the Shaker church.

"Sometimes when it's Pentecost Sunday, and we're all gathered together and we read about the room suddenly being seized and everybody shaking, I think, 'wouldn't it be great if we all began to have that Spirit?' But we don't.

"If it's God's will for it to happen, it will happen," says Sister Frances, seen here at the podium in the Meeting House.

"When people ask me, 'Do Shakers shake in church?' it makes it sound like it's a deliberate effort and it isn't. Unless that power takes you over you're not going to shake. If it's God's will for it to happen, then it will happen. I don't think that my wanting it to happen will make it happen. You can't make yourself have this manifestation."

"We don't have the same spirit that they had in the early days. Things change. At that time, people were desperately seeking to know more about the Spirit of God, of the Christ, of Mother Ann. Perhaps they needed it more.

"Perhaps it will come back. I don't know."

A single row of four tiny chairs rests against a wall in the Winter Chapel of the Dwelling House. This is where the youngest children sat, apparently transfixed, when Sister Eliza began "whirling" under the power of the Holy Spirit in 1938. The last time children who were in the care of Shakers used these chairs was in the 1950s.

Chosen Faith, Chosen Land

Work
Hands to work, hearts to God

Work begins long before daylight for the Brothers at Chosen Land where the needs of the Family's livestock, the sheep and the cattle, come first. Brother Arnold is dwarfed by the imposing Great Ox Barn, and metaphorically, the enormous daily demands of their agrarian way of life.

Therefore, my dear brothers, stand firm. Let nothing move you. Always give yourselves fully to the work of the Lord, because you know that your labor in the Lord is not in vain.

1 CORINTHIANS 15:57-58

Much of the work required to keep Chosen Land operational is done by either volunteers, such as Robert Emlen of Rhode Island, or hired help.

Open for Business

There is a "dual nature" to a Shaker's work. The duality of their labor is represented by either physical or spiritual effort, and when they make the two become one, they have put their "hands to work, their hearts to God," as Mother Ann bade them.

The amount of work necessary to keep Chosen Land open and operating is formidable. The Shakers can't do it all themselves, especially the manual labor, so they hire people from the community to help with everything, from tending the apple orchard to cleaning the ninety-eight windows of the Dwelling House.

Each Shaker has duties at Chosen Land "according to strength and ability" as stated in their literature; they are "all working for each, and each for all," and they believe there is dignity in all labor. Daily responsibilities require each Shaker to move in different directions and with different people. But there is one task that requires a united monumental effort, and that is the constant, defense-oriented public relations battle waged on a world stage to remind people that America's Shakers are open for business.

The problem is simple. Most people think there are no more Shakers. They think they're all dead, hence the erroneous assumption that the faith is dead, as well. How and why this happened is more complex.

An unfortunate series of events gave rise to a lie that to this day conceals the truth about present-day life at Chosen Land—a lie that deeply impacted the American Shaker experience. It is a bitter story, marking the darkest chapter in the history of the Shakers' 20th-century existence. It is the story of a schism that began simmering in the early 1960s between the last two Shaker villages in the country, Canterbury in New Hampshire and Sabbathday Lake (Chosen Land) in Maine. The schism, the first ever within the history of Shakerism, erupted when the New Hampshire Shakers called for the Maine Shakers

Though only a few Shakers call the Dwelling House home now, it was built to house a burgeoning population of Believers.

The Shakers' Scottish Highlanders are an old breed that are rapidly gaining popularity among cattlemen due to their outstanding ability to thrive in harsh conditions.

to follow their lead and close the Shaker Church to new members, essentially writing the faith's obituary. The Maine Shakers strongly protested, and eventually rebelled. They paid a dear price for their defiance, and history has yet to determine how high a price was exacted.

An "apostate" is someone who embraces a faith with passion and commitment, then later denounces it publicly with equal zeal. Wherever there have been Shakers, there have been apostates.

The most famous Shaker apostate was Mary Dyer, a woman who joined the Enfield (New Hampshire) Shakers in 1813. She brought her husband and their five children into the community as well. Convinced she had not found the salvation she was searching for, Mary left two years later—with her family in tow. That's when all hell broke loose. Her husband wanted to stay and keep the children with him. Mary was devastated. She tried everything,

Work

including asking the state legislature to enact laws to break up Shaker communities. The sensational story made headlines around the world. Mary's last, albeit unsuccessful, resort was a two-year public-speaking campaign across America lambasting the Shakers and the faith. Mary never got her family back, but her very public crusade against the Shaker faith and its Believers drew blood.

There are no Shaker apostates the likes of Mary Dyer in today's world, but there is another force at work, a subversive one, that continues to threaten the viability of the faith. "They are of a different ilk today," says Brother Arnold of

Brothers Arnold and Wayne walk through the woods of Chosen Land toward the shimmering light reflecting off the surface of Sabbathday Lake.

modern-day apostates, adding that it gets worse every time a death or departure thins the ranks of the faithful. "And ever since then we constantly get the 'They're all dead.'"

The apostate Brother Arnold is referring to is today's mainstream media and its fascination with the demise of Shakerism—each reporter seemingly set on getting the scoop on America's last Shakers. An endless stream of headlines and news reports heralding the end has not slowed down for decades. The myths and misperceptions created by such sloppy journalism are an insult to the Shakers and a disservice to the public at large.

The time has come for people to learn the truth, this time from the Shakers themselves. It's also time to put the nail in the coffin of Ken and Amy Stechler Burns's *The Shakers: Hands to Work, Hearts to God* (1987; 1999), a well-researched, sympathetic look at Shaker history. Unfortunately, the book, along with the Burns's 1984 PBS film of the same title, is primarily responsible for the myth that Shakerism died.

The Burns's book and film took the side of the Shakers living at Canterbury who closed the church, fearing new members would be more interested in the Shaker financial fortunes than their faith. There were other issues as well, but that was the crux of their position. The only other active Shaker community at the time was Chosen Land, whose members wanted to keep the church open to potential converts. The Canterbury Shakers in 1961 were made up of four elderly women. The Chosen Land Shakers consisted of Sisters Mildred Barker, Elsie McCool, Frances Carr, Marie Burgess, Minnie Greene, Eleanor Philbrook, Della Haskell, Ethel Peacock, Christine Greenwood, Olive Dobson, Eva Libby, Elizabeth Dunn, and Brother Delmer Wilson. There were also several young girls who were still living there as wards of the Shakers. (Theodore Johnson began living at Chosen Land in May of 1960, but he did not sign the Covenant to become a Shaker until a few years later.)

In support of their position, the Maine Shakers cited the Church's Covenant of 1830 that states, ". . . the door must be kept open for the admission of new members." A line in the sand had been drawn, and Shakers and non-Shakers alike lined up waiting for the other shoe to drop. The controversy chipped away for years at the "unity" between the two villages, a concept so essential to Shakerism, until there was nothing left but cause for a showdown.

The Canterbury Shakers won the battle in 1972 because they controlled the purse strings. Canterbury was much stronger financially than Chosen Land—which for many years was perched on the edge of poverty. The Canterbury Shakers denounced the Maine Shakers and essentially cut

"For Thine is the Kingdom." Aerial view of Chosen Land. The original road (Route 26) was cut by Shakers in the late 1700s from their village to the nearby town of Gray. In 2003, the State of Maine redirected and widened the road, so it now bypasses the heart of Chosen Land, making their cluster of historic structures much less visible to passing motorists. © CHUCK FEIL

Chosen Faith, Chosen Land

them off financially, leaving the women and Brother Ted withering on a vine burdened by the weight of a village they could no longer afford. It was a devastating time.

The tragedy of the Burns's work is that they filmed and interviewed the Shakers at Chosen Land in 1981 for inclusion in their documentary, but nearly all of it was edited out, including the fact that three Shaker men were living there at the time. In the end, viewers were clearly left with the impression that Canterbury was the only Shaker village remaining and the four aged women living there had closed the church. It was a huge mistake by all accounts, including many academics, a mistake made more apparent with the passing of time.

Canterbury closed in 1992 with the death of the last Shaker Sister living there. The 694-acre site grew to become a thriving, well-managed living history museum attracting more than 60,000 visitors annually. Chosen Land, on the other hand, remains an active Shaker Village occupied by living Shakers who carry on the tradition of the faith in an ecumenical spirit that permits them to worship with people "of the world."

A later edition of the Burns's book attempts to correct the unfortunate imbalance of truth, but it was too little, too late, and the documentary continues to air nationally and internationally and is in video libraries around the world. With this book, I am attempting to set the record straight for the simple reason that Sister Frances asked for my help back on that fateful Sunday in 1998. I had no idea what I was getting into.

I received several thousand dollars in funding for this project from the New Hampshire Humanities Council in 2003, most of which went to scholar-guided research I conducted, and the filming of the interviews with the Shakers at Chosen Land. Ironically, Ken Burns sat on the Board of Trustees of that organization when they voted unanimously to support my work to correct the record. God works in mysterious ways, indeed.

The Schism
Sister Frances Carr

"No church should be closed to anyone. Shakerism is alive and well here at Sabbathday Lake. People have just never gotten the message that it is."
—Sister Frances

The acrimonious schism left a deep and indelible mark on the heart of Sister Frances, who was in her 40s and 50s when the painful drama played itself out. The long-running feud between the two villages constitutes the only issue that ever caused Sister Frances to think about leaving the faith.

She says fault lines between the two communities first appeared in the late 1950s, when the Canterbury Sisters, most of them elderly, turned over much of their affairs to a group of Manchester, New Hampshire, lawyers. "I think the legal system took advantage of them," she says, adding the Sisters had become convinced that anyone who wanted to join the Shaker faith was really only interested in what the Shakers had, such as their land, buildings, money, and much sought-after antiques. Millions of dollars were reportedly at stake. The only way to protect the Shaker fortune from 'gold diggers' posing as potential converts, as the story is told, was for the Canterbury Shakers to announce there would be no new members. The announcement set the wheels in motion for their substantial assets to be put into a trust to be used to support the then living Shakers.

"They told us to close our doors, not to take in anyone else," said Sister Frances. "We refused to do that. We said, 'You don't close the doors of a church. This is God's work.' It didn't make any sense. We refused at great suffering." And that's when the other shoe dropped. In 1972 the Canterbury Sisters "cut off a great deal of the financial assets that were ours, legally," she says, adding, "It was a very hard, difficult time." They stopped sending Chosen Land its share of the funds, an estimated $3,000 per month, although they did continue to pay taxes and insurance. They also provided a meager $10-a-week allowance for each Shaker Sister, but nothing for Brother Ted, who, they ruled years earlier, was not even a "real" Shaker. Insult had been added to the injury of poverty. But the worst was yet to come.

The next blow, perhaps fatal, came with the airing, beginning in 1984 and continuing to this day, of the Ken Burns documentary that states unequivocally, "these (the aged Canterbury women) are the last Shakers."

The popular film left people with the impression that it was impossible to be a Shaker. "I heard that for so many years," says Sister Frances. "People say, 'I never realized there's a Shaker community. I thought they were dead.' That's the word that got out and it went everywhere. It turned people away. They thought there was no chance of coming here and becoming a Shaker. No one ever had the opportunity to give it a try because the media just constantly…," her words were choked off by emotional memories.

Over time, the myth grew and spread, assuming a life of its own. Sister Frances claims tourists who visited Canterbury's Shaker Museum in the 1970s and 1980s were told no one was ever going to be able to become a Shaker again. She says the same misinformation was given to people at other historic Shaker Village museums, as well. "I had been to South Union and Pleasant Hill [Shaker Villages] in Kentucky doing workshops and giving lectures. A friend of mine went to Pleasant Hill a while after I had been there, and he heard a person working there say, 'Well, of course there aren't any Shakers now.' And my friend spoke up and said, 'What about Sister Frances?' And they said, 'Well, she came over on that rickety boat hundreds of years ago.' So even being there personally didn't change the myth," said Sister Frances, who found no comfort, under the circumstances, in being mistaken for Mother Ann.

She is pragmatic about the ramifications of the myth, which continues to be perpetuated. "I sometimes think museum operators want us to be in the past. That's what they want. But we are a Shaker community. We do not want to become just a museum."

Brother Arnold

Brother Arnold agrees there are people who would be glad to see the end of Shakerism, particularly those who might prosper from its demise.

"We've been battling this for a very long time. Longer than I've been a Shaker," he says. They approach the problem from many angles. "We print, we publish, we allow interviews, we have our own Web site, we have a museum, and we have an open community. I don't know what else we can do. The thing of it is," he said with remarkable candor, "is that Shakers have never mattered as much as the people who write about Shakers. So the best we can do is hope that people who have questions will write or call, and we can set them right and give them the facts."

Brother Arnold, working in his office in the Dwelling House is surrounded by a clutter of tasks awaiting his attention.

Material Culture
Brother Arnold

"What I'm doing is 're-seating' an old Shaker chair that someone brought us. The original seat had worn out. It was made at Mt. Lebanon (Shaker Village, N.Y.), probably in the 1920s. It's something we've done here for a long time. What I've done is I've saved the original seat because it adds to the overall value of the chair, and if somebody at some point later on wants to go and restore it, they have a right to, and it's all there. They just have to take a lot of care, and no one would be able to sit in the chair again.

"I was taught this twenty-five years ago when I first came here and I've been doing it ever since. The money we'll realize will go into the community's coffers and will do something to help everybody."

Above and top right: Brother Arnold seating or "listing" a Shaker chair for a client. It is a unique skill he learned upon arriving at Chosen Land in 1977. He and Brother Wayne also carry on the Shaker tradition of making oval wooden boxes that are sold to the public in the Shaker Store.

Today's Shakers do not mince words when it comes to their feelings about the world's people and their obsession with collecting items of Shaker material culture—often paying exorbitant sums. Oprah Winfrey, for example, paid $200,000 at auction in 1990 for a piece of Shaker furniture. Brother Arnold remembers his reaction to the news:

"Anybody has the right to do with their money as they wish. She wasn't bidding against herself. There were plenty of other people.

"It would be very easy for me to be judgmental and give you something glib, but the truth is you can't look into people's hearts and know.

"If that's what starts people thinking about the name of the Shakers and they like it, chances are they're going to start researching it and they're going to try to find out more. If Shakerism will always be with us, so will our material culture. It's not as enduring as the faith, but it comes pretty close because people will take care of it. If it is a beginning point for people to start to understand the faith, it is a good thing.

"My opinion is it's of the world and for the world. I really don't care about the material culture."

Sister Frances

"There's been a great surge of interest in Shaker artifacts, Shaker furniture. And there have been many auctions at which things have gone for huge amounts. Just recently there was a little Shaker basket that had originally belonged here at Sabbathday Lake. It was given to a person by Sister Eleanor. That went up at auction and it brought $55,000. It just boggles the mind.

"We go back to another huge auction when (Oprah Winfrey) paid a huge amount for some Shaker artifacts. I was terribly disgusted. I thought of the hundreds and hundreds of people that would feed, or helping people who are ill. It's ridiculous.

"I think it would be a wonderful idea if people who have obtained a Shaker artifact or piece of furniture, for I dare say a few dollars, would return these things to the communities from where they came. Even some of the museums. . . it would be better for them to have these things than to just put them into a private collection."

Contrary to popular belief, Shakers do not shun technology. In fact, they welcome technological advances if they help them work more efficiently.

Work as Worship

Work is central to Shaker life, and working together as they often do helps create an interdependency that has characterized life in Shaker communities from the very beginning.

Shakers welcome mechanical and technological progress. They use computers, tractors, electric mixers, cell phones, whatever they can afford or invent that enables them to quickly and efficiently get the job done. Historically they were prolific inventors. Their list of time-saving devices is long and impressive and includes the flat broom, the circular saw, the clothespin, a threshing machine, and the first garden seeds to be sold in small paper packets. A washing machine patented by the Shakers won a gold medal in 1876 at the Centennial Exposition.

Today's Shakers hold no patents, but they are an industrious group to say the least. They maintain a tree farm, apple orchard, vegetable gardens, a commercial herb garden, hayfields, pastures, a flock of sheep and other livestock. They operate a store, library, museum, and an Internet e-commerce Web site *www.maineshakers.com.*

Sister Frances begins her day in the kitchen, at 6:30 a.m. She starts by making breakfast for the Family. "And then I spend two or three hours every morning preparing the noon meal," she says of their main meal, which on most days means feeding 12 to 14 people.

Among the Shakers' numerous inventions is this yarn-swift, which eliminates the need for someone else's hands to help with winding. © BRIAN VANDEN BRINK.

A typical noon meal prepared by Sister Frances serves 12–14 people(Shakers, staff and researchers) and consists of several homemade courses, including dessert. "We like to invite people to break bread with us because it is the best way for everyone in the community to visit," she says.

Work

Old metal dust pan and brush hanging on red brick wall in mudroom of Dwelling House.

"We always feed the staff members (3), and then we have our librarian and our secretary. If someone is in the library working there we generally invite them to the meal also." It is an enormous undertaking for a woman her age, but she does it with grace, charm, and even a touch of style. She pays close attention to how the colors and textures of the prepared foods look next to each other as she displays them on one of several long Shaker-made tables in the dining room.

"Hands to work, hearts to God," is Mother Ann's most famous aphorism, and for Sister Frances it holds special meaning. "I've always felt that religion and work go hand in hand, and by putting our hands to work and giving our hearts to God, God blesses that work, in my opinion. And so perhaps God blessed my work as a cook, because I have been very happy in that ever since."

"Work as worship is just another way of putting hands to work and heart to God," says Brother Arnold. His daily chores take him to the barn first thing in the morning and to minding the cash register and other duties in the Shaker Store during tourist season when necessary. Next, a mountain of administrative tasks waits in his office in the Dwelling House, then it's back to the barn again in a cycle that repeats itself for 12 to 14 hours every day.

He feels the world's people misunderstand what Shakers mean when they use the word "labor." "To the world," he explains, "laboring would be like a laborer, somebody who goes out to do work. That's what we're doing, but we're doing it both physically and spiritually. When you put it into spiritual terms, anything you do has the potential of being an act of worship if you are in the spirit of doing it. So if you're sweeping the floor, that has the potential of not being a task of drudgery, but rather, it's a way of serving God because it's keeping your home clean and it's helping other people. Everything we do is supposed to be done in that spirit."

Brother Wayne works side-by-side with Brother Arnold when it comes to taking care of the animals and the two barns, but he alone is primarily responsible for haying and maintaining the fields, mowing the grass and plowing the

Sister Frances, holding the handle of a broom, still sweeps the floor of the kitchen daily despite her age and the arthritis that has set into her fingers.

Daily chores for the Brothers include a thorough sweeping of the restored 1830 Stable & Ox Barn. Brother Wayne says this task is a daily reminder of the story behind "The Sweeping Gift."

mountains of snow that fall on the village every winter. More than 100 inches fell during 2007.

Brother Wayne also records the Family's daily activities in a journal. It is an important duty that generations of Shakers before him performed. These journals, which are kept private for fifty years, are first-person accounts of Shaker daily life. They include a variety of information, everything from mundane weather reports to the comings and goings of visitors, and from the drama of fires to the details of Shaker departures. Brother Wayne, for example, would have recorded the Shaker's perspective on the production of this book and planned film. The journals are used by historians as primary source material to help the general public understand what real Shaker life was like during a particular era.

Sister June works in the library and assists Sister Frances in the kitchen. She is also responsible for keeping the dining room running efficiently; dishes, silverware, and napkins in order; tabletops washed clean; crumbs off the floor. She loves to feed the starlings, mourning doves, and blue jays that perch on the back porch railing of the Dwelling House. "Sister June's greatest gift," says Sister Frances, "is her love of God's creation. She loves every single animal, every bird that flies, and she has a beautiful faith."

A tiny English House sparrow is "hidden in plain sight"—like the Spirit itself—as it perches on a sill in the stable.

Chosen Faith, Chosen Land

World

In the world, but not of the world

A shaft of sunlight illuminates the rungs of a ladder in a loft of the Great Ox Barn built in 1830. The tangible presence of the spirit, "hidden in plain sight," according to many world's people who have been there, permeates Chosen Land.

The world and its desires pass away, but the man who does the will of God lives forever.

1 JOHN 2:16–18

Eyes fixed on the television and a tissue in her hand for more tears yet to fall, Sister Frances watches and processes the unforgettable events of September 11, 2001.

E verybody remembers where they were on September 11, 2001, the day terrorists carried out the single most deadly attack on American soil in the history of our country. I was with the Shakers at Chosen Land, and it was the last place on earth I wanted to be that day.

Eleven days earlier I had left my job as a broadcast reporter and anchorwoman for the Portland, Maine, ABC affiliate to start a video production company. I'd spent twenty years in the business. I had a month's worth of unused vacation/comp time that I was burning, so technically I was still employed as a broadcast journalist when the World Trade Center was hit. A reporter's instinct kicks in fast when something like that happens, and I immediately called the newsroom and offered my help. By noon that day, I realized I would play no part in reporting what would have been the biggest story of my career because the networks took complete control of the airwaves with "wall-to-wall" coverage. There was no room, especially during the first eight hours of that nightmarish day, for local coverage. So I did what came naturally. I grabbed my 35mm camera and an old video recorder and drove seven miles to Chosen Land, where I had recently begun documenting the lives of the Shakers.

We did what millions of people around the globe did that day, we watched TV, tears in our eyes and fear on our minds, wondering what in the world would happen next.

Shakers, as Christians, are called to live "in" the world, meaning they're here to fulfill God's will and purpose for them, but they're warned not to be "of" the world by becoming polluted or tainted by worldly actions or desires that God does not bless—such as lust, consumerism, jealousy, pride, and violence.

One of the original reasons Shaker societies were communal in design was to keep temptation at bay, to keep the bad things "of" the world at a safe distance from Believers who lived "in" the world.

In fact, it was not unusual for many 18th- and 19th-century Shakers to have no contact with the outside world at all. There were even symbolic cleansing rituals for Shakers who, by necessity, were forced to mingle with the world's people, such as those who conducted trade with or were buyers of provisions for the community.

That kind of separation is so far removed from the reality of Shaker life in the 21st century that it exists virtually in theory only. Modern technology, from laptops to cell phones to televisions, brings the bad things "of the world" quickly and directly into the heart of the Shakers' lives—9/11 is a perfect example.

I wondered, as I sat with them in their family room, Sister Frances clutching a Kleenex and Brother Arnold knitting on the couch, what these peace-promoting pacifists were thinking as they watched the towers implode with people still inside, melting to the ground below. What were they thinking when that toxic cloud of debris rolled through the streets of Manhattan, sucking the life out of everything in its path?

Would America's living Shakers have the spiritual strength to do what Jesus would do? What Mother Ann would do? Would they pray for their enemies; could they turn the other cheek? I wanted to know if these peace-loving Shakers could truly resist the worldly urge to hate and to retaliate, claiming the one true God, their God, was on their side. Or would they pray as I did that day, to be on God's side in the impending global war to come?

Sister June wasn't with us that evening. Someone said she wasn't feeling well and had gone to her room. I think she'd had enough. The reactions of the other Shakers may surprise you.

The Shakers on 9/11

"Oh my God. O dear, dear, dear..." Sister Frances said it softly, repeatedly. She was admittedly in shock that day, like most of us.

This "Dove with Two Rings" gift drawing by an anonymous Shaker speaks to Shaker pacifism and their hope for peace. Courtesy of Hancock Shaker Village, Pittsfield, Massachusetts.

JL: "When you realized the country was under attack, what did you think?"

SF: "At first I couldn't make it seem real. I saw it on television. I heard all the reports, and for most of the morning I kept thinking, 'this is not really happening.' I was in a state of shock and disbelief."

JL: "There's a lot of feeling in the world right now that it's time to retaliate."

SF: "I don't know. Even that's difficult, too. As Shakers we don't believe in taking anyone's life. We don't believe in the death penalty. As a Shaker Sister I don't believe in abortion, because to me it's a way of taking a life. I was saying to Brother Arnold this evening, 'We're horrified. We see this dreadful thing that has happened, and we know someone needs to be punished for it. And yet, I almost have a sense of dismay thinking that we're probably going to. The country is going to take some military action, and a lot of people…" Her voice trailed off. She was clearly thinking about how the U.S. would respond, and the lives yet to be taken.

"It would be one thing if the people responsible for this were severely punished, to the point of annihilating them. But that's not possible without taking innocent people as well. It's a very tough situation to be in."

JL: "What should we learn about pacifism from this?"

SF: "If only the whole world would begin to take that stand, and strive for peace. As we often say, peace has to begin in individuals, in the community, then spread out to the world. I'm probably talking about something that most people will never have an understanding of, but to us here in this community it is a possibility.

"We're all going to be praying very hard, and have been praying all day. Whenever something we've heard strikes us particularly, and we feel so terribly concerned for all those who have lost their lives, and their families, we pray. And we pray that they will find peace in their lives, and that the whole world will someday come to a knowing of peace."

JL: "It's my understanding that you (Shakers) try not to feel hatred or even bitterness toward the people who flew those planes into the World Trade Center. Do you?"

SF: "That is a difficult question. I'm not sure what I feel. Again, most of what I feel is disbelief that this could possibly happen. I'm not sure if bitterness is what I feel. Again, I have to say, it's disbelief and horror about what has happened.

"Mother Ann, when she was being persecuted, and horribly misused, said that she did not have bitterness towards her enemy. She just prayed, and tried to follow the example of Christ, and ask for forgiveness. I don't think I feel that way right this moment, but again, I can just say I feel a horrible sense of disbelief, just horrible."

JL: "Are you concerned for the world's safety?"

SF: "Absolutely. I never thought this could happen. I was a young teenager during the Second World War, and I lost a brother in that war. I knew war was horrible. But for us in the United States it's never been this close, and today it truly seems like war has come to America."

JL: "What would you tell President Bush?"

SF: "To do the very best to get the opinions and help of everybody, regardless of what party they belong to, anyone who has experience in leading this country. Depend on what they have to say. And do a great deal of praying for guidance."

Brother Arnold

Brother Arnold was sitting on the couch next to the television. His feet, in worn socks, were resting on an old leather ottoman. He was knitting a light blue scarf, using wool from their sheep. When complete, the scarf would be offered for sale in their store at the upcoming annual Christmas Fair.

JL: "How did you come to know that America was under attack?"

BA: "We had a phone call this morning. They told us to turn on the television, so we did. I called Sister Frances right away. During that time period, from the plane hitting the first tower, a second plane came, and we saw it hit the second tower. We knew certainly that two planes hitting two towers in fifteen minutes couldn't possibly be an accident."

JL: "When did you pray? How soon after you realized what happened."

BA: "I think we prayed right away, as soon as we saw the first one hit, whether it was an accident or not. We had to pray for the people involved, on the plane and in the towers."

JL: "Were you ever afraid here?"

Brother Arnold, knitting a scarf to be sold in the Shaker store, and Brother Wayne sit quiet and still while watching developing news coverage of 9/11.

BA: "Nay. I don't think any terrorists even know Maine exists."

JL: "What should we understand about today with regard to pacifism?"

BA: "Pacifism isn't easy. And you know, a belief in peace is not easy. You have to actively pursue it as the Gospel tells us. In the Psalms it says, 'Seek peace and pursue it.' And that's what it's all about. It would be very easy to give in to anger, to hatred, to a sadness that would lead you to those other elements, as well, which are all of darkness and not of light. God is all light.

"All we're called to do is practice incredible compassion. I think our first feelings and understandings, our prayers, our compassion, have to go out to the innocent victims, those people who just happened to be in the wrong place at the wrong time.

"We also have to recognize that there is definitely evil in this world, and that evil will do all in its power to make bad things happen. So we can't be a part of that. We can't be a part of the evil or the darkness, or those things that are not of God. Rather, we have to be that which is of God, which is love, which is compassion, which is caring. I took a great deal to heart from all those people who said they couldn't do anything, and they felt very helpless, but the one thing they could do was give blood. And all those blood banks started to fill up with willing volunteers."

JL: "What about wars that people, governments, or nations carry out in the name of God?"

BA: "Well, of course, that's not God. People unfortunately abuse the name of God and try to pervert God's word and His will by practicing war upon each other, but God has nothing to do with war, at all. The Prince of Peace we say, as Christians, [is who] we follow. Therefore we can't be a part of war."

Brother Arnold cradles a lamb in 1986. Although his decision to become a Shaker meant he would never father children, Family members describe him as paternal and nurturing. Sister Frances says whenever she is ill, Brother Arnold makes sure she stays in bed and brings her hot soup. "He is just such a good person. He has many gifts, "she adds.

"Tree of Love" gift drawing. Courtesy Hancock Shaker Village, Pittsfield, Massachusetts.

JL: "Tell me why you believe so profoundly in pacifism."

BA: "If you're a Christian you can't do anything else. Jesus constantly tells us that 'those who live by the sword will die by the sword,' and, 'My followers are not of this world.' We have to wage peace. If we are part of this creation, and we recognize all here on this planet as truly our brothers and sisters, how could you wage such war on your own family? Especially with a parent as we have in our Father/Mother God who is all love, who has shown us nothing but love, and expects out of us nothing more than to show back that same love."

JL: "How will you feel tomorrow, if it hasn't happened already, if we learn that the U.S. has launched air strikes against Afganistan, which is where we believe Osama Bin Laden has been hiding?"

BA: "I'll feel awful, really, in one sense. But in the other sense, I also realize that nations aren't governed by the same principals that I espouse as an individual, or that we espouse as a community. Rather, they are governed by a whole other set of rules and regulations. They're going to do what they feel is right."

JL: "Is there any prophecy here, anything that you believe in, that is happening that the world maybe doesn't understand with regard to the Christian faith?"

BA: "Nay, nay. These are not the end days. This is not the end of the world. This is just one more sign of what man can do to man, and what happens when we let evil take over our lives."

JL: "And how would you define that evil?"

BA: "That evil tells you it is right to kill other people, that you can take down anybody at anytime and you're justified because you say, 'God tells me it's the right thing to do.'"

JL: "But aren't there occasions, though, when..."

BA: "Killing is never right. Killing is never right. It is never right."

JL: "You won't find it anywhere in the Bible?"

BA: "Well, you might find it in the Old Testament, but you will never find it in the New Testament."

JL: "What do you want our community to know about your thoughts about pacifism and today's attack on America?"

BA: "The only thing we Shakers do is pray. We pray for resolution to all things. But mostly what we pray for are the individuals who have been hurt. Those who have died are already with God. I think the living are the ones who really need our prayers, those who have been maimed either in body or mind, or both. They need a lot of healing. They need a lot of understanding and compassion. Those are the people I pray most fervently for."

Brother Wayne

Brother Wayne cried. I saw him wipe a tear from his eye as he watched people running from the toxic cloud that formed when one of the towers collapsed.

Sister Frances speaking at The Pacifist Memorial in Sherborn, Massachusetts at the dedication of a plaque in honor of Mother Ann Lee. Brother's Wayne and Arnold (l to r) are also in attendance. The memorial "bears witness to humanity's pursuit of justice and peace through nonviolence and love." A statue of Mahatma Gandhi stands at the center of the memorial; radiating outward are six brick walls engraved with the names of and quotations from sixty peacemakers including Jesus, Sojourner Truth, Anne Frank, Martin Luther King Jr., St. Francis of Assisi, and Mother Ann Lee, whose plaque reads:

"O Holy Father, I will be a child of peace and purity.
For well I know thy hand will bless the seeker after righteousness."

Courtesy of Rae Hoopes

JL: "When you realized today that this was a terrorist attack on the United States, what were you thinking?"

BW: "Initially, just disbelief. It was just so surreal to see a jetliner crashing into the World Trade Center, and to also think that this was done deliberately. It was just startling. It always seems that terrorism is something so remote. It's horrible when people lose their lives in such senseless, violent acts. But now it has struck close to home. While we are Shakers, we are also Americans, so this is an attack on us, as well. It's disturbing."

JL: "How do you reconcile your feelings of wanting to protect your country, yet not harboring hatred toward the people who did this?"

BW: "If you let hatred and anger control your decisions, then you're going to end up at the same level they are at. As a civilized society, we're supposed to be rational and make our decisions carefully. If we allow this overwhelming urge for revenge to take over our national consciousness, then we're going to be just like the terrorists. We're going to go into Afghanistan or the Sudan, or wherever Bin Laden is hiding out, and we're going to kill thousands of people who are not involved in these activities, just as thousands of Americans died today. There is obviously this national need to bring some sort of justice to the perpetrators and organizers of the crime, but you have to somehow figure out where that fuzzy line is between justice and revenge."

JL: "What do you think we should do?"

BW: "I don't know. I have a lot of emotions about this, and I know what as a Christian I'm supposed to think."

JL: "What is that?"

BW: "About forgiving and not seeking revenge, and turning the other cheek. But there's also the practical experience of, you know, if you don't stand up to a bully they continue to bully. So again, it's that whole idea of the rule of law and rule of justice, as opposed to the rule of revenge and an eye for an eye. I think, perhaps, there is some way to do it. But, we, as the leader of the free world and a civilized society, have to tread carefully that we don't fall into the same plot because emotions are running very high in the country and we could do a lot of bad things."

JL: "Do you think that bad things will happen, things our country will condone, because of what happened today?"

BW: "I hope not. It could. Obviously, the reason the terrorists wanted to strike at us is because they believe our country has acted unjustly. So this is their way of striking back at their perceived injustice. I think if we pursue the whole idea of vengeance, we're just going to be kicking the hornet's nest more. So it's a Catch-22. I don't think there are any simple answers. It's going to require prayer, contemplation, and a careful weighing of our decisions."

JL: "Do you think prayer can turn this around?"

BW: "I think so, if people are open. I think sometimes people pray for answers, but they don't listen to the answer because it's not what they are thinking in their heart and mind."

JL: "When you go to bed tonight, what will you pray for?"

Today's Shakers share their message through numerous outreach programs and public events. Here, Master Gardener Betsy Golan gives a tour of the Shakers' gardens to a group of local women.
© JERRY AND MARCY MONKMAN/ECOPHOTOGRAPHY

BW: "I'll pray for wisdom for the leaders involved in these events. I'll certainly pray for the victims. I'll pray in a spirit of hopefulness that we won't get caught up in the passion of revenge."

JL: "But you couldn't and wouldn't fight?"

BW: "I don't know. That's a very hard question. I've never been asked to. Also, I'm a little old for the draft. I would hope that I would always do the right thing. I know that's a guarded answer, but that's the best answer I can give."

JL: "What do you want the community to know about how difficult it is to be a pacifist in a world where the push of a button can blow us up in a second, and how close we live to the edge?"

BW: "I don't think in our witness to pacifism we honestly believe we're going to stop all the wars. But I do think people need to bear witness to the fact that there are alternatives to using violence for conflict resolution, that sometimes there's an awful lot of pride in the way nations comport their foreign affairs that aggravate other people. I think what we need to do is to have a wiser foreign policy, be more mature and responsible, and realize that violence is not always the answer. It doesn't ever solve problems, it only creates new ones.

"If we start attacking civilians, then we end up being just like the terrorists. I think our leaders have a lot of difficult decisions to make. I really hope that there will be a spirit of wisdom for them, and that they can do what's right."

An array of signs shows the variety of events the Shakers use to increase awareness.

Strategic Advance

Shaker history is a story of advance and retreat vis-à-vis the world. While at various times in the past great energy was directed at building walls around Believers, the contemporary community at Chosen Land is very outward facing, even dressing like "world's people" for the most part. Today the boundaries of their village are far more permeable than ever before. America's Shakers are now in a period of strategic advance. They are careful about the kind of contact they have with the world, reaching out to people with a targeted approach that serves their needs. The general thinking is, "the more the world's people come to know and appreciate us through our culture, the better they will come to an understanding of our faith, and perhaps find that it appeals to them spiritually." It is a very subtle form of proselytizing in an age, unlike the past, when they no longer need to close ranks out of fear of persecution. "We're not going to go out on street corners and preach. That doesn't really work," said Brother Wayne. "I think the Shakers found out, and other groups found out, you can go and get people all stirred up, but sooner or later the fire dies out and they're gone. I think we need to find people who are already looking. I think being open, whether having our museum, doing interviews, speaking engagements and the like—and we've traveled as far as Western Europe to do things—it just lets people know that we're here, and that we have worship services open. You never know who's going to drop through. You never know."

The Shakers' strategic advance begins with the village itself. It operates as a museum four and a half months out of the year, attracting an estimated 10,000 people each season. A 2008 exhibit, "The Human & The Eternal," featured more than one hundred items from the museum's folk art collection, highlighting artistic expressions by Shakers from the 1800s into the late 20th century. Objects displayed in the popular exhibit included Shaker gift

Christmas Fair volunteers proudly display proceeds from the "White Elephant" sale. 100% of these funds go toward gifts for needy local families.

View from the orchard at Chosen Land to the ox barn. © Jerry and Marcy Monkman/Ecophotography

World

drawings, oval boxes, hooked rugs, painted frames, intricately carved wooden shelves, paintings on glass, and hand-stitched quilts and samplers.

The Library at Chosen Land houses the world's largest collection of manuscripts, books, and artifacts on the history of Maine Shakers and attracts its own scholarly crowd, many of whom are in the business, academic, and otherwise, of promoting the knowledge and preservation of all things Shaker.

The push to advance public awareness about the viability of contemporary Shakerism reached a crescendo in 1994, when the Shakers joined forces with the internationally acclaimed Boston Camerata to produce a CD of Shaker songs. Joel Cohen, the director of the a cappella group and an expert on Shaker hymnody, asked the Shakers to sing with the Camerata for the CD, and they agreed. Titled *Simple Gifts,* it is a moving collection of a variety of distinctive tunes ranging from ballads to chants and marches. He is a close friend of the Shakers, and a well-respected scholar of Shaker hymnody. He spent countless hours in the Shaker Library transcribing hundreds of spirituals and chants from archived manuscripts, narrowing the selection down to thirty-six songs. The recording is considered an excellent example of early American hymnody, and the Shakers' voices can be clearly heard in the group tunes, especially that of Sister Frances.

The album was recorded in the Meeting House and was partly funded by the National Endowment for the Arts (NEA). The Shakers even traveled to Boston in 1996 where they sang with the Camerata before a sold-out crowd at the historic Faneuil Hall. It was a poignant performance that brought the audience to their feet at the show's conclusion.

The Shakers also interact with the "world's people" at regularly scheduled special events such as music performances, fall "Apple Saturday" tours of the orchard, craft fairs showcasing hand-made baskets made by Maine Native Americans, and a vigorous schedule of Shaker-inspired workshops.

Young members of the "Friends of the Shakers" display the fruits of their labors while learning the value of community service at Fall Work Day at Chosen Land in 2000.

One event, in particular, draws thousands of people from all over New England to Chosen Land on the first Saturday in December. It's the annual "Shaker Christmas Fair," now in its 31st year. Early-birds stand single file along Route. 26, waiting sometimes up to two hours—often huddling for warmth in subfreezing temperatures with complete strangers—for the Shakers to open the doors of their store. The fair is geared toward holiday shoppers looking for unique gifts such as Shaker–made jellies, fruitcakes, breads, wreaths, and oval boxes. It is typically one of the Shakers' most profitable events of the year. They even offer a "White Elephant" room stocked to the ceiling with items donated by "world's people." One hundred percent of the proceeds from White Elephant sales goes toward helping needy local families during the holidays. They usually generate around $2,000 and the Shakers themselves shop for the gifts they donate to their less fortunate neighbors.

The success of these events, designed not only to generate revenue for the Shaker coffers, but also interest in Shakerism itself, would not be possible without incredible support from a little-known group of people called the Friends of the Shakers.

The "Friends"
Getting By With a Lot of Their Help

Today's Shakers are surrounded and supported by a larger community called the "Friends of the Shakers". The non-profit, all-volunteer group was founded in 1974 to assist the Shakers at Chosen Land in matters both temporal and spiritual, and over the years they have helped with everything from restoring historic buildings to raking leaves. Several women helped out in the kitchen when Sister Frances was hospitalized following knee surgery. They

A plentiful organic harvest plucked from branches at Chosen Land to nourish a community of believers, Shaker and non-Shaker alike, united by the belief that living 'in the world, but not of the world' is possible

The Friends of the Shakers—a nonprofit organization—assist the Shakers in innumerable ways, from spring and fall cleanup to restoring buildings to helping out in the kitchen.

grieve with the Shakers when there is a death in the Family, offering support and comfort.

These are the trusted "world's people" the Shakers call upon during times of need, which have increased of late as the number of Shakers has decreased. They are their confidants, advisors, true friends, and spiritual brethren.

Although they have not signed the Covenant to become actual Shakers, the faith completes them by enriching their lives. They come from all walks of life with not much in common other than a passion for the Shakers and their beliefs.

There are an estimated 550 dues-paying members of the steadily increasing group. They come from around the world, although most live in the New England region. They attend Sunday Meeting with the Shakers when they can, form Shaker study groups in communities where there are clusters of "Friends," and publish a newsletter three times a year called *The Clarion* that keeps members connected and up to date on happenings at Chosen Land.

The "Friends of the Shakers" have repeatedly demonstrated remarkable fundraising skills, rallying around the family financially in matters great and small. The most significant achievement in the history of the organization was raising $207,000 for the Trust For Public Land's successful $3.6 million campaign to preserve and protect Chosen Land forever.

From money to muscle, "Friends" play a crucial role in taking care of the physical aspects of Chosen Land, its grounds and gardens, and eighteen historic buildings, the "newest" of which is the 100-year-old garage built in 1910. (The Shakers, incidentally, were the first people in the town of New Gloucester to own a car. The year was 1909, the vehicle was a Selden, bought for $2,100.)

The magnitude of chores is more than the Shakers themselves could ever accomplish, especially since the Sisters are advanced in age. In an effort to help, several dozen Friends converge on the village twice a year, in the spring and fall, work gloves in hand, to do whatever is asked of them. Young and old alike wash windows, clear debris from roadside culverts, harvest fruit and vegetables, split and replant bulbs, repair broken screen doors, sanitize tin containers for the Shaker's herb business, rake, weed, and clean. In the words of one Friend, "we come expecting the To-Do List from Hell." And like days gone by, there is dignity in the labor of all, which is assigned equally and according to ability. No regard is paid to educational background, economic or social status, age, or gender. This is how fully functioning Shaker communities used to operate, and the egalitarian system continues to work well.

The original wood stove in the 1794 Meeting House is no longer used. When temperatures drop, Shaker worship services are held across the street in the Winter Chapel, on the 2nd floor of the Dwelling House.

The 1903 water tower at Chosen Land is now the most visible structure to a motorist passing by on busy Route 26.

The Friends' most important function, however, is one they may not even be aware of. They are all goodwill ambassadors for the faith, shattering myths and misperceptions about the viability of Shakerism among people in the greater community. Friends are the ones who explain the faith's nuances to other people. They often encourage family members, coworkers, and friends to join them at Chosen Land, and that's how the "circle" widens. They give talks at local schools and libraries. They write books and articles about Shakerism, its history and material culture. Friends have been referred to as Shaker "apologists" by some because of how closely they guard the Family, even screening out individuals who may not have the Shakers' best interests at heart. But to those who matter most, they are highly regarded as dedicated members of the Shakers' extended Family who can be counted upon to do whatever it takes to help keep the faith alive.

Boot scrapers buried in a granite step leading to the Meeting House. The simple, practical devices ensure that cleanliness is next to Godliness.

Chosen Faith, Chosen Land

Future

Simple and free

A new day dawns over Sabbathday Lake.

"While we look not at the things which are seen, but at the things which are not seen: for the things which are seen are temporal; but the things which are not seen are eternal."

2 Corinthians 4:18

What Lies Ahead

The Shaker faith began with one woman, Mother Ann Lee, experiencing a mystical oneness with the Christ Spirit. It grew to become the church of all those who sought that same oneness, and, by simply seeking, found it. "The second coming of Christ is in the Church," said Mother Ann. The Church is nothing other than the "mystical body of Christ" whose eventual triumph is in the Millennium, which has come.

That Mother Ann suffered death from the effects of mob violence against her is a martyrdom today's Shakers recall as if it happened only yesterday. Her slow, quiet death, surrounded by Believers, her last words to them, the later exhumation that revealed a shattered skull, and the fragment of her apron, silently remind today's Shakers that at its core her message was, and may always remain, a dangerous one. It demands separation from the world and an overwhelming attention to living the life Christ lived—the Kingdom Life.

Living the Kingdom life may invite ridicule and persecution, for it holds a mirror up to the world and reveals things the world may not want to see. It is—and will always be—a radical challenge to live as Christ lived. To deny that, to attempt to escape it, is to miss the message Christ taught.

That with time Shakers interpreted and re-interpreted the meaning of Mother Ann's message should come as no surprise. She told them to seek the Spirit from within, which they have done. It is not surprising, then, that the four who have spoken through the pages of this book have different versions of the future of the faith. They offer a spectrum of beliefs, with equal conviction, as to why they feel the faith is not over.

To Brother Wayne, it matters less whether spiritual seeking is done as a Shaker than that it is done at all. What matters to him is that it is a spiritual labor; that it continues the ongoing relationship between God and man.

"We ask God to lead people here. We believe there is going to be a future. Hopefully, other people are going to come and embrace the Gospel, and we're here for that purpose. We live our lives and hope we'll be an example for others, and others will come. It might be that no one will live here again at Chosen Land, but if someone lives this life, yet calls themselves something else, aren't they still doing the same work? And the work of God isn't just about people like Mother Ann, it's about a continuing ongoing interaction between God and man."

To Sister Frances, however, "its terribly important that a core of Shakers always be at Chosen Land. I pray earnestly that God will show us what to do. That He will tell us how we are to continue to keep His/Her word going here at Chosen Land. Beyond that I cannot prophesy, I can only tell you what I hope— that there has to always be a core of Shakers in this place or it will not be a Shaker community."

She agrees with Brother Wayne that you do not necessarily need to live at Chosen Land to live the Kingdom life. "I don't think for a minute that I have to be here, where I am now living, in order to be a Shaker. Once a Shaker, always a Shaker, I feel. And I could be a Shaker in Ohio."

She then recalled a beautiful story about Mother Ann that was recorded in the *Testimonies*.

One day in Massachusetts, Mother Ann and a very young Sister were going through an orchard. It was the beginning of the ripening season. Some of the apples were still very small, but it was an ongoing process, and Mother looked at the apples and said to the young Sister, 'Now, look at this apple tree. Some of these apples will grow larger, but then fall off. And others will continue to grow and become larger still, and then they will fall off. But some will go through, grow into full, large apples and continue to be on this tree. And that is the way with souls. There are some who will set out on the way and they will fall early on. Others will go on even farther in the way, but unfortunately, they will fall away. But then there are those who will grow through to the end. I pray that I am one of those who will go through to the end.

Mother Ann likened the souls of Believers to apples on the branch—some fall off early, some grow larger and then, fall off, and some go through to the end, becoming the richest fruit of the harvest. "I pray that I am one of those who will go through to the end," says Sister Frances.

Brother Arnold is pragmatic. "Being an Elder in the community, I'm also, unfortunately, responsible for bringing others into the faith and to sustain them and see that faith grow."

"How are you doing on that?" I asked, already knowing the answer.

Laughing, at himself mostly, he said, "I don't know that I'm doing all that well. I pray on that every day. My waking prayers always encompass doing God's will, not my will, and that I be given the patience and wisdom to grow and to see this community grow."

Brother Arnold shares a moment of affection with his beloved dog Habakkuk. He named the family pet after the Biblical prophet who foresaw impending doom during the last days of Judah. Habakkuk's message to people of faith was to wait with patience and trust in God's plan in spite of dark days ahead.

Chosen Faith, Chosen Land

Sister June takes a different view. To her, what is important is that the beliefs themselves continue. "Whatever happens to us here, I think the beliefs will continue because they're important to people in general, and their relationship to God, and their living for God. Personally, I hope the life here will continue as it is now; but we'll have to wait and see what God wants."

She, too, believes the essence of being a Shaker is not dependent upon a communal society. "You don't have to live in a community necessarily to be a Shaker."

The Shaker faith has certainly changed over the years; it was meant to. The word "faith" itself is a verb; it is active, alive, it is contemporary. But one constant remains, and that is Mother Ann Lee. Her spirit is alive. She spoke from the ethereal world to Frances, Arnold, Wayne, and June, asking them to join her on a mission to ignite souls. They responded, surrendered, to her message.

"Yea, I love Mother," says Brother Arnold.

Many people come through Chosen Land and are changed by it. Some go back out into the world, even those who lived there for a long time. Are they as much Shakers as the "covenanted" ones? I believe so.

Will the requirement of living in community be one of the spiritual "travels" out of which Shakers will emerge in a new form? Will other Shaker tenets give way to new meaning? I believe so.

Mother Ann herself shared a vision for the future of the faith more than 225 years ago. It is a message as full of promise today as it was back then.

"This gospel will go to the end of the world, and it
will not be propagated so much by preaching, as
by the good works of the people."

—Mother Ann Lee

A Message of Hope

I asked each Shaker what was their "message to the world."

"God is present. God is there. God is in us. He's in you; He's in me. She is there."

—Sister Frances

"God is love, that's all."

—Sister June

"I think that Shakerism is alive. We are still an active community. It's a great way of life."

—Brother Wayne

"That it is an individual quest. Mother said, close to the end of her life, 'I am but one person. I have done my work. Now you must do yours.' That really sums up what the life is supposed to be. The people have to do the work themselves."

—Brother Arnold

"We'll have to wait and see what God wants." —Sister June.

Simple and Free

A few years ago my fifteen-year-old twin sons asked me if they could attend a non-denominational Christian summer camp. I was thrilled to learn of their interest, having mentioned the same camp a year before, only to have my suggestion shot down. So I said it was fine. One of the boys then tossed the camp's application form on my desk and asked, "What church do we belong to?"

I looked up and said, "What?"

"They want to know what church we belong to," he said. "Does Shaker church count?"

It was a good question. People knew we worshiped there, but were we real "members?" I wasn't sure my teenagers wanted to be known as non-covenanted members of the Shaker church, but it truly is the only church we attend on a regular basis. I paused for a moment, which felt like an eternity, then replied as casually as I could, "Write down The United Society of Believers, in New Gloucester."

"What's that?" Tyler asked.

"It the official name for the Shaker church," I said. "I'll write that and you're good to go." I picked up a pen, hesitated a moment, and wrote it down—twice—once on each boy's application. I looked up to see their reaction, but they had already left the room. No big deal.

For me, however, it was a defining moment.

My kids tagged along with me to Chosen Land ever since they were toddlers. They grew up listening to people at Sunday Meeting testify about their "Father/Mother" God. They learned the old Shaker songs orally, the way generations of Shaker's had before them. They help with chores on spring and fall workdays. They raised the standard for volunteer "biscuit runners" at the Shaker's annual Christmas Fair. They saw novitiates come and go. They attended the wake for Sister Marie in 2001. It's the only church community they know.

My children were just fine letting people know they're members of The United Society of Believers, the Shakers. I, on the other hand, am ashamed to admit the incident left me uncomfortable. The act of writing it down on a piece of paper made it so real, so "official," so "out there" for everyone to see. Why did my hand hesitate?

It took a while for me to figure it out, but I now realize my inner conflict boiled down to this: I was *subconsciously* guilty of buying into the generally

A Victorian-era Shaker bedroom on display in the Ministry Shop reflects the somewhat monastic nature of the faith life. © Brian Vanden Brink.

held belief that being a Shaker is "weird," and I didn't want people to think I was weird, or that my children were weird. I had suffered enough criticism from my own family for going to Shaker church and I didn't want to hear it from anyone else. Additionally, I knew of several "Friends of the Shakers" who had also been criticized or ridiculed, including one person who was written out of a will due to her affiliation with the Shakers. I didn't have the courage then to publicly admit my beliefs are aligned with contemporary Shakerism. Now, I do. I've matured personally and spiritually.

What I've learned is that our society does not value the Shaker faith, despite the fact that we value highly their material culture. How do I know this is true? Because the only thing the Shakers are trying to do at Chosen Land is to live the way Jesus Christ did—as a celibate, a communalist, and a pacifist. Given the choice to live like Jesus, most people wouldn't or couldn't do it, even though they proclaim his name and his way. I'm convinced that if Jesus returned to earth today, bringing the same message of love and peace that he preached two millennia ago, our society would ignore him all over again—or worse. We are still not ready as a society, but our society does appear to be in transition spiritually, and therein lies hope for the future.

Shortly after I came to this conclusion I discovered a Master's thesis on Shakerism in the library at Chosen Land, written in 1991 by David L.nRichards for the University of Southern Maine's New England Studies Program. His work, entitled "Reconstructing the Boundaries of Community: The Sabbathday Lake Shakers in the Post-Bellum Era, 1870–1920," revealed a disturbing portrait of America—a so-called "Christian" nation. In the summary of his 206-page essay he writes,

Those head counters and eulogists who persist in confusing change with decline should consider the following. If Shakerism should cease to exist some day, it will not be because of the suicide of celibacy. More likely it will be the result of the inhospitality, and sometimes outright hostility, of an often antithetical dominant culture which has made the fixed Shaker principles of community, celibacy, confession, and pacifism seem like romantic old-fashioned absurdities. In a world which still has inadequate and ineffective methods of caring for the ill-fed, ill-clothed, ill-housed, and just plain ill; in a world hell-bent on pushing Malthusian demographic theory to its apocalyptic limit; in a world which has fought two World Wars and numerous minor 'police actions' since the Civil War; in a world which has lived for the past half century under the constant threat of nuclear annihilation; it is chilling to think that there is no place for the United Society of Believers in Christ's Second Appearing. If that is indeed the case, future historians may have to reassess which society really went into decline after 1860.

The tale of my personal faith journey is over. What I discovered at Chosen Land liberated me by turning my world upside down. In retrospect, it was all so simple. I feel a little like Dorothy, who traveled all the way to Oz only to realize what she searched for could be found at home, in her heart.

The author at Chosen Land in 2003 sitting on a slab of granite in front of the Great Ox Barn going over notes and research materials in preparation for a 3-hour, on-camera interview with Brother Wayne. © REBECCA JEFFRIES.

Epilogue: November 2006

I must have been the last person to find out. I hadn't been to Sunday Meeting in a few weeks, maybe it was a few months, I don't know. I hadn't been there in a while. Everyone was acting strange after Meeting. It was November, all the "summer Shakers" had gone. There were only five or six of us there besides the Shakers. Brother Wayne was missing. "What's going on?" I asked one of the regulars. "Why is everybody acting so strange?" She moved in close and whispered, "You need to ask Brother Arnold. It's about Brother Wayne."

"He left earlier this week," said Brother Arnold.

"What do you mean, 'he left?'" I asked, though I already knew the answer.

"He left the church," he said, emphasizing the word "church." "He ran off with a woman—a reporter from the *Boston Globe* who was up here this summer doing a story on us." He said it with an uncharacteristic edge to his voice.

I was speechless for a moment or two. Then I started crying. Brother Arnold just stood there, slowly shaking his head from side to side. In a flash I realized he

must have witnessed a virtual cascade of tears and emotion from the other people he'd told about Wayne over the past week. Exhausted and overwhelmed with anxiety and confusion about what to do next, he added, "We've know about it for months. We just didn't know when he was actually going to leave."

I was so upset that I had to get out of there. I felt like someone had just ripped out part of my heart. I missed Brother Wayne already. He had been my spiritual guide, pulling me along as he pushed himself forward in search of the elusive inner light in uncharted theological territory. Soul-searching is like mountain climbing; it's a lot of hard work, but well worth the effort once you reach the peak. I doubt Brother Wayne knew how profoundly his perspective shaped my own beliefs. I had so much more to learn from him, through him. I felt as though I needed him to help me finish my journey. I loved him like a brother, but that day I hated him.

Brother Wayne, in silhouette, leaving the Meeting House in September 2003 following Sunday Meeting. His departure was noted with brevity:

"On November 21st Wayne Smith, a Brother for many years, left the Community. We wish him well in his new life."

"Home Notes" by Sister Frances Carr, *The Clarion,* Spring 2007

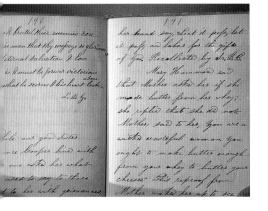

Driving home, all I could think about was how difficult it had been three years earlier for him to answer my questions about celibacy. Was it a foreshadowing? Was he thinking about leaving even back then? Did he answer my questions honestly at the time?

Over the next few months, I did what Mother Ann asked her children to do whenever there was an unresolved grievance. I "labored for a gift of God" through prayer. I asked for wisdom and guidance on the issue of Wayne's departure and my bitter feelings toward him. Forgiveness never came easy to me in the past, but this time was different because I was different. I was eventually able to "let it pass" and move on. I am so grateful to have learned this important lesson, but I will always be amazed by the circumstance that preceded it.

I soon returned to climbing spiritual mountains—this time alone, but with greater strength and deeper insight and more courage. I began spending less time at Chosen Land, feeling less need for guidance. My Shaker mentors had taught me well.

The most important lesson I learned from America's living Shakers was that coincidence had nothing to do with me finding the little-traveled dirt road leading to Chosen Land back in 1992. That was, in Sister Frances' words that day, a "God-incident." I had labored nearly all my adult life for a richer, deeper understanding of the nature and image of God, and my prayers were answered.

Finally, I would like to believe the Shakers' prayers were, in some small way, also answered when I began working on this project back in October 2000. They desperately want the world to know that the doors of their church are open, that their faith resonates with contemporary meaning. I believe the Spirit brought us together, in the most remarkable way, to fulfill both our needs.

To Sister Frances—thank you for giving me the gift of yourself: you are and always will be my earthly spiritual mother; loving me unconditionally while demanding nothing but the best of me. Trust me. Know my intentions

Left: "Let it pass, let it pass, and labor for the gift of God." Mother Ann Lee.

All things considered, it seems appropriate, if not important, to include one of the last questions I asked a Shaker during my weeklong visit to Chosen Land. To Brother Arnold I asked, "What is your favorite saying of Mother Ann?" To which he replied, "One quote in particular strikes me, and that is:

'The young sisters came to the aged and good Sister Deliverance Cooper and asked her what did Mother Ann do when people came with grievances? And Sister Deliverance responded that she often would see Mother gently pick up her hand and lightly shake it and wave it about, and say, 'Let it pass, let it pass, and labor for the gift of God.' And why that one has always stuck with me is because you see how petty our grievances are. And that rather instead of looking at them and criticizing them, and especially in Mother's case having to choose a side, she chose the right side, which was neither of them, because they were both probably wrong. And, I think in all of our grievances we are both probably wrong, too. But rather, we are to look to the greater thing, which is that gift of God, and that would give us the discernment, the wisdom and the understanding and the answer.

"I have to remember that every day. That's why I picked it out, because I *do* have to remember it every day."

I offer love and optimism to my spiritual mentors—America's 21st-century Shakers—and gratitude to the Spirit that brought us together in the most remarkable way.

are good. Do not worry or be anxious about the future. To Sister June, my Sister in the faith and a kindred "spiritualist"—thank you for reminding me constantly that the Spirit lives within me. I feel it now, every day. And I can see it in other people, too, the way you did when you were with your mother in Boston all those years ago. God bless you, always and forever. To Brother Arnold—thank you for sharing with me the gift of your brilliant, no-nonsense mind. You make me think. Your dogged determination and spiritual courage inspires me, more than you know. You are bold, yet tender; wise, yet still curious. The Spirit has big plans for you.

Epilogue

May the gate to Chosen Land remain forever unlocked.

And to Wayne —thank you for showing me the wisdom and power of progressive revelation. I promise to keep working on my relationship with God. I won't lean on anyone but the Spirit. Keep the faith, my brother in Christ.

January 2008

Chosen Land is alive and thriving, but it is also changing, as it should. Joining and departing have been ongoing features of Shaker history from the beginning, and the years covered in this book are no exception. Additional proof of this is found in a young woman named Sacha Tovani who had been corresponding with the Shakers for a couple of years about "trying the life," and she is now the community's newest member. She spent ten days with the family in April of 2007, and was invited back to begin her novitiate period in June, which she did. "Sister" Sacha, as she is now called, is a pretty, intelligent, articulate and positively passionate woman. She has not yet signed the Covenant making her an "official" Shaker, that won't occur until her novitiate period is over. Till then, I wish her "love, more love," a line from an old Shaker hymn.

Journalists, from the middle of the last century to filmmaker Ken Burns in the 1980s to contemporary reporters working in the modern media, have all predicted the demise of the American Shaker experience. All have been proven wrong. There is nothing more satisfying to a storyteller than finding the ending to a great tale. Documentation, however, is not storytelling. Its rewards lie elsewhere. Simply put: the story this book tells is not over.

Author's Note:

Chosen Faith, Chosen Land is a great story about a fascinating group of people at a critical crossroad in American history. It is also a great history book that took shape under the guidance of several of the most respected Shaker scholars in America.

The interviews with the Shakers conducted for this book and a planned documentary were done during the second week of October 2003 in various locations at Chosen Land. The interviews were videotaped and transcribed. I presented a copy of the full transcript to the Shakers shortly after for their review, as is common with oral history projects of this nature. The Shakers made no additions, modifications, or corrections.

In addition, I, and photojournalists Olof and Sharyn Ekbergh, shot footage and conducted interviews with non-Shakers at Chosen Land "for background" on eleven separate occasions between 2000 and 2001.

The Shakers' comments as they appear in this book have been edited for clarity and general ease of reading. Much attention, however, was given to preserving the context of their words.

There are instances throughout this book where I felt it was necessary and appropriate for pacing, substance, and tone to portray the text as a transcript of the actual conversation. In those cases, the letters "JL" indicate my question or comment, followed by a Shaker's response. "SF" is Sister Frances, "BA" is Brother Arnold, "BW" is Brother Wayne, and "SJ" is Sister June.

Eight Shaker scholars, including Brother Arnold Hadd, attended a seminar I conducted at Canterbury Shaker Village and Museum in New Hampshire, on June 20th, 2003. The goal was to help guide my research and preparation for the upcoming Shaker interviews. These scholars, among many others who played a role in supporting this project, are listed at the end of this book.

Copies of the full transcript, the full videotaped interviews, and additional footage gathered at Chosen Land from 2000 - 2003 will be made publicly available for research purposes in the collections of the Sabbathday Lake Shaker Library and Museum in New Gloucester, Maine, and the University of New Hampshire Special Collections Shaker Unit in Durham, New Hampshire.

Acknowledgements

Writing a book about what is likely the world's smallest religion would have been impossible without enormous help and support, for which I am truly grateful. I estimate more than 100 people and organizations assisted me in ways big and small over many years, but those listed here, in alphabetical order, are primarily responsible for helping me bring the important story of America's 21st-century Shakers to the "world's people."

Tina Agren, the librarian at Sabbathday Lake Shaker Village Library.

Betsy Connor Bowen, my partner on this project for many years.

Cynthia Close, Executive Director, Documentary Education Resources, Boston, Massachusetts, the first person from "the business world" to support this project.

Sharyn & Olof Ekbergh, WestSide AV, North Conway, New Hampshire, my filmmaking partners, long-time financial supporters of this project, and dear friends.

Chris Funkhouser, Vice President, American Public Television, Boston, Massachusetts, long-time supporter.

Rebecca Jeffries, my sister, assistant, and long-time supporter.

Abby Johnston, my graphic artist at Upala Press in Portland, Maine.

Laurie Kahn Leavitt, filmmaker, supporter, and mentor.

Flo Morse, journalist/author, original scholar on this project, and friend.

The Friends of the Shakers .

The Maine Center for Integrated Rehabilitation,
the doctors and therapists who helped me rebuild my body and reinvent my mind.

The Maine Humanities Council.

The New Hampshire Humanities Council.

Michael Steere, my editor at Down East.

Jeff Toorish, my photographer, former co-anchor, and long-time friend.

John Viehman, my publisher at Down East.

Professor David Watters, The University of New Hampshire, my primary scholar/advisor for nearly a decade, and the original editor of this book.

Gerard C. Wertkin, Shaker scholar and author, Director Emeritus, American Folk Art Museum, New York, and author of the foreword to this book.

Selected Bibliography

Print

Andrews, Edward Deming. *The People Called Shakers*. New York, NY: Dover Publications, 1953.

Brewer, Priscilla J. *Shaker Communities, Shaker Lives*. Hanover, NH: University Press of New England, 1986.

Campion, Nardi Reeder. *Mother Ann Lee, Morning Star of the Shakers*. Hanover, NH: University Press of New England, 1976.

Carr, Sister Frances A. *Growing Up Shaker*. Sabbathday Lake, ME: The United Society of Shakers, 1994.

DeWolfe, Elizabeth A. *Shaking the Faith*. New York, NY: Palgrave, 2002.

[Rufus Bishop, compiler]. *Testimonies of the Life, Character, Revelations and Doctrines of Mother Ann Lee, and the Elders with her, Through whom the Word of Eternal Life was opened in this day, of Christ's Second Appearing, Collected from Living Witnesses, In Union with the Church*. 1816. Shaker Library, New Gloucester, ME.

Francis, Richard. *Ann the Word*. New York, NY: Arcade Publishing, 2000.

Garrett, Clarke. *Origins of the Shakers*. Baltimore and London: The Johns Hopkins University Press, 1987.

Green, Calvin and Seth Y. Wells, *A Summary View of the Millennial Church of United Society of Believers Commonly Called Shakers*. Albany, NY: The United Society, 1848.

Humez, Jean M. *Mother's First-Born Daughters*. Bloomington, IN: Indiana University Press, 1993.

Mack, Phyllis. *Visionary Women: Ecstatic Prophecy in Seventeenth-Century England*. Los Angeles, CA and London: University of California Press, 1992.

Marini, Stephen A. *Radical Sects of Revolutionary New England*. Cambridge, MA: Harvard University Press, 1999.

Mathewson, Angell J. "Reminiscences." *Letters to his brother Jeffrey, 1781–1813*. New York Public Library, New York.

Melcher, Marguerite Fellows. *The Shaker Adventure*. Old Chatham, NY: The Shaker Museum, 1941.

Mercadante, Linda A. *Gender Doctrine & God*. Nashville, TN: Abingdon Press, 1990.

Morin, France. *Heavenly Visions: Shaker Gift Drawings and Gift Songs*. New York, NY and Los Angeles, CA: University of Minnesota Press, 2001.

Morse, Flo. *The Shakers and the World's People*. Hanover, NH: University Press of New England, 1987.

Patterson, Daniel W. *The Shaker Spiritual*. Princeton, NJ: Princeton University Press, 1979.

Rathbun, Reuben. *Reasons Offered for Leaving the Shakers*. Pittsfield, MA: Chester Smith, 1800.

Rathbun, Reuben. A Letter From Daniel Rathbun. Springfield, MA: 1785.

Rathbun, Valentine. A Brief Account of a Religious Scheme Taught and Propagated by a Number of EUROPEANS, who lately lived in a Place called NISQUEUNIA, in the State of New-York, but now residing in HARVARD, Commonwealth of MASSACHUSETTS, commonly called, SHAKING QUAKERS. Worcester, MA: 1782.

Stein, Stephen J. *The Shaker Experience in America*. New Haven and London: Yale University Press. 1992.

Taylor, Amos. *A Narrative of the Strange Principles, Conduct and Character of the People Known by the Name of Shakers*. Worcester, MA: 1782.

Thurman, Suzanne R. "O Sisters Ain't You Happy?" Syracuse, NY: Syracuse University Press, 2002.

Wertkin, Gerard C. *The Four Seasons of Shaker Life*. New York, NY: Simon and Schuster, 1986.

White, Anna, and Leila S. Taylor. *Shakerism: Its Meaning and Message*. Columbus, OH: Fred J. Heer Press, 1905.

Interviews Conducted by the Author

Carpenter, Sister June. Shaker/Sabbathday Lake Shaker Village, ME. Three-hour on-camera interview, 7 October 2003.

Carr, Sister Frances A. Shaker Eldress/Sabbathday Lake Shaker Village, ME. Four-hour on-camera interview, 7 & 9 October 2003.

Haagen, Mary Ann. Visiting Professor, Dartmouth College/Director, Shaker Singers. Personal Interview. 29 & 30 April 2003. Enfield, New Hampshire.

Hadd, Brother Arnold. Shaker Elder/Sabbathday Lake Shaker Village, ME. Personal interview. 6 May 2003. Topic: Ann Lee & Shaker creed/theology.

Hadd, Brother Arnold. Shaker Elder/Sabbathday Lake Shaker Village, ME. Four-hour on-camera interview, 6 & 9 October 2003.

Humez, Jean. Professor, University of Massachusetts, Boston. Author. Personal interview. 2 May 2003.

Morse, Flo. Author. Personal interview. 9 August 2002. New Gloucester, Maine.

Smith, Wayne. Shaker/Sabbathday Lake Shaker Village, ME. Four-hour on-camera interview, 6 & 9 October 2003.

Watters, David. Professor/Director, The Center for New England Culture. Personal interview. 4 March 2003 and 17 July 2003. University of New Hampshire, Durham, NH.

Watters, David, et al. Shaker Scholar Seminar for Mother Ann Project. 20 June 2003. Canterbury Shaker Village, NH.

Correspondence

Garrett, Clarke. Professor of History Emeritus, Dickinson College. October 2002.

Marini, Steve A. Professor of Religion, Wellesley College. 7 & 9 November 2001.

Stein, Stephen J. Chairman of the Department of Religious Studies, Indiana University. January 2003.

Scholars and Advisors

Leonard Brooks – Executive Director, Shaker Village Library, Sabbathday Lake, Maine. Principal research conducted under his guidance at this important research facility.

Joel Cohen – Preeminent authority on Shaker music and hymnody. Director, the Boston Cameratta.

Michael Graham – Curator, The Sabbathday Lake Shaker Museum, New Gloucester, Maine. As curator, Graham is responsible for evaluating, interpreting, and displaying 235 years of Shaker history.

Jerry Grant – Director of Research and Library Services at the Shaker Village Museum and Library, Old Chatham, NY. Grant is an author, editor, and publisher of several respected Shaker books, articles, and newsletters. He also lectures widely on the subject.

Mary Ann Haagen – Visiting Scholar of Dance at Dartmouth College, Hanover, NH. Haagen is a well-respected Shaker expert and founder/director of the SHAKER SINGERS, a living-history performance group dedicated to preserving the historical accuracy of early Shaker song and dance. The SHAKER SINGERS perform regionally. Haagen is also the Musical Director/Producer of two CDs of Shaker songs, *O Hear Their Music Ring* and *All at Home*.

Jean Humez – Professor of Women's Studies at the University of Massachusetts, Boston. She is the author of several books and articles on women and religion, including *Mother's First-Born Daughters,* 1993 (Indiana University Press), which chronicles the contributions made by women, especially Ann Lee, during the first 70 years of Shakerism in this country.

Sharon Koomler – Director of the Shaker Museum and Library, Old Chatham and New Lebanon, New York. Koomler is also an author who has extensive knowledge of Shaker gift drawings. Her books on Shakerism, including *Seen and Received* and *Shaker Style,* are popular among academics as well as general audiences.

Flo Morse – Author of four popular books about the Shakers, including *The Shakers and the World's People, 1980* (University Press of New England.)

Stephen J. Stein – Professor of Religious Studies, Adjunct Professor of History and Chairman of the Department of Religious Studies at Indiana University. Prof. Stein is considered this country's quintessential Shaker scholar. His 1992 award-winning *The Shaker Experience in America* was the first-ever general history of the Shakers from their origins in 18th century England to the present day.

Scott Swank – President, Canterbury Shaker Village, a national historic landmark site and museum with 25 original buildings situated on 694 acres. Swank is a leading Shaker historian and the author of several books on Shaker material culture, including *Shaker Life, Art and Architecture*.

Darryl Thompson – Shaker historian, author, and lecturer. Thompson is considered an authority on Shaker research materials.

David H. Watters – Professor of English and Director, Center for New England Culture at The University of New Hampshire. Professor Watters is a Shaker expert who lectures regularly to academic and community audiences.

Index

A
Andrews, Edward Demming, 135–136
Apostate, 27, 145

B
Barker, Mildred, 36–37, 38–39, 50, 96, 110, 128
Beldon, Ricardo, 54
Bible, 113
Bloom, Harold, 17–18
Brackett, Joseph, 98, 122–123
Burgess, Marie, 72
Burns, Amy Stechler, 147
Burns, Ken, 11–12, 147, 149

C
Canterbury Shaker Village, 144, 147–148, 149, 150–152
Celibacy, 60, 104, 106–107
Charismatic Movement, 121
Charity, 71–72
Christology, 111
Cohoon, Hannah, 64, 97, 121
Communalism, 107–109
Concise Statement, 29, 102, 103
Confession, 109–111
Covenant, 176, 194

D
Dwelling House, 80–83
Dyer, Mary, 145–146

E
Ecstatic Worship, 20, 120, 136–142
Era of Manifestations, 30, 114, 121

F
Father/Mother God, 43, 97, 101, 187
Friends of the Shakers, 175–178, 180

G
Gift Drawings, 121, 135–136
Gnosticism, 17, 18
Great Awakening, 20, 21
Green, Calvin, 104
Green, Minnie, 72

H
Haagen, Mary Ann, 138
Hocknell, John, 25

J
Jeffers, Eliza, 140
Johnson, Moses, 83–84, 85
Johnson, Theodore, 38–40, 54, 55, 56, 57, 87, 96, 97, 98

K
Kingdom Life, 68, 70, 72, 106, 116, 183, 185

L
Lee, Ann, 14, 16–31, 34, 35–36, 94–95, 100, 108, 109, 112, 182–183, 185
Library, 39–40, 86–88, 174
"Life in the Christ Spirit," 96, 112

M
Material culture, 88, 135–136, 152–154
Meacham, Joseph, 29, 102, 104, 108
Meeting House, 83–85
Millennial Laws, 110
Museum, 88

N
Novitiate, 59

P
Pacifism, 161–167, 171
Pagels, Elaine, 17
Patterson, Daniel, 37
Peace Abbey, 167
Pentecostalism, 121
Postmodernism, 13–14, 127
Progressive Revelation, 101–104, 113, 194

Q
Quakers, 20

R
Richards, David L., 189

S
Sabbathday Lake, 90
Sawyer, Otis, 86, 88
Schism, 144, 150–152
Second Coming of Christ, 25, 35, 94–95, 103, 112
Sedgley, Iona, 88
Shaker Manifesto, 100
"Simple Gifts," 121

Spiritualism, 114
Standerin, Abraham, 20–21
Stickney, Prudence, 49, 140

T
Testimonies, 16, 30, 109, 183
Tiffany, Charles, 72
Trust for Public Land, 89, 92, 177

U
United Society of Believers, 24, 84, 187, 190

W
Wardley Society, 20
Whittaker, James, 23, 25, 29, 96, 106, 108
Wilson, Delmer, 52
World's People, 127, 172, 174, 176, 178
Wright, Lucy, 29